HINDUISM:

A Path to Inner Peace

An Analytical Perspective

Mohan R. Pandey

Cover photograph of lotus by M. Pandey

ISBN: 148119710X
ISBN-13: 9781481197106

Library of Congress Control Number: 2012923348
CreateSpace Independent Publishing Platform
North Charleston, South Carolina

Printed in the United States of America

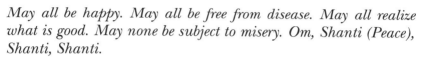

May all be happy. May all be free from disease. May all realize what is good. May none be subject to misery. Om, Shanti (Peace), Shanti, Shanti.

—Hindu Peace Chant

Peace in the world depends on peace in the heart of individuals.

—Dalai Lama

Blessed are the peacemakers: for they shall be called the children of God.

—Matthew 5:9

All that we are is the result of what we have thought. The mind is everything. What we think, we become.

—Buddha

As he thinketh in his heart, so is he.

—Proverbs 23:7

A man becomes what he thinks. This is the eternal secret.

—Maitreya Upanishad 1.9

CONTENTS

1

ESSENCE

May your inner soul be the fountainhead of divine light.

—Yajur Veda

For many in the West, Hinduism can seem rather confusing. For those who are used to having one God and one holy book that covers everything about the faith, where the rituals are structured, organized, and formal, where people wear their "Sunday best" while attending weekly church services, and even the weddings have a rehearsal, the flexibility and informality of Hinduism can appear chaotic.

With multitudes of scriptures, multiple paths to the Supreme Being, rituals that seem mind-boggling at times, and with the heavy emphasis on symbolism—many gods and goddesses with multiple hands, some with multiple heads, some with divine looks, to some downright scary—Hinduism can bewilder many.

Actually, Hinduism is very simple. It believes in a Supreme Being or the divine essence, which is the Supreme Soul.[1] It believes that everyone has the potential to connect with that divine essence by his or her own efforts.

The physical body, which changes with time, is transient. Hinduism believes that the Supreme Soul is the only thing that is unchanging and eternal.

The physical body, which is composed of the basic elements of the universe, becomes alive when the soul enters it. When the soul leaves the body, one dies and the physical body reverts to the basic elements of the universe.

Hinduism considers the Supreme Soul to be the ultimate truth or the reality. It believes that the materialistic world, the senses, the mind, and the ego prevent people from recognizing this ultimate reality. To realize the ultimate truth, one needs to create a lasting stillness within.

The parable some use is if one lets a glass of muddy water sit still, eventually one can see through the clear water. Likewise, if one can subdue the ego and stop the senses from churning the mind, one will be able to discover that stillness. Hinduism is all about inner transformation—stop the churning and attain inner peace.

Hinduism believes that when one achieves that lasting stillness or the inner peace, the individual soul connects with the Supreme Soul. It is as if the soul suddenly starts to transmit a signal that had remained dormant for a long time—a signal that is preprogrammed to transmit at a special frequency that will resonate with the divine frequency.

For the Hindus, the whole purpose of existence is to develop the lasting inner peace and connect with the Supreme Soul or the divine essence. Rituals, symbols, scriptures, and the multiple paths are mere tools or means to get to the ultimate truth. Hinduism allows utmost flexibility in the pursuit of inner peace.

If one is not able to develop inner peace and connect with that divine essence in one's lifetime, one goes through the cycle of reincarnation or rebirth. Upon attaining the lasting inner peace, the individual soul connects with the Supreme Soul and the cycle of rebirth stops; one attains *moksha* or *mukti*, "connection with the Supreme Soul and liberation from the cycle of rebirth."

Rather than believing, Hinduism is about being and becoming. It is about being peaceful and becoming *mukta*, "one who has attained *mukti* or *moksha*."

It is similar to Buddhism, whose goal is to attain *nirvana*. *Moksha* and *nirvana* are similar; both are about attaining the inner peace and being freed from rebirth; except in *nirvana*, Buddha did not get into the individual soul and was silent on the Supreme Soul.

In Hinduism, humanity's problem is ignorance of the ultimate reality or the Supreme Soul. Hinduism does not regard ignorance as bliss; it considers knowledge as bliss. Wisdom and knowledge are greatly valued.

Hinduism recognizes the attractions of materialism. It does not want its followers to feel left out of the entire materialistic experience. Hinduism believes in the importance of developing one's full potential, making money, having a family, and enjoying all the materialistic pleasures. However, with the passage of time it gradually wants to wean them out of their attachment to materialism.

Once one has experienced the pleasures and the associated pains of the materialistic world for several decades, Hinduism believes the mind will be ready to free itself from the attachment to materialism and focus on the stillness within.

Hinduism divides a person's life into stages to get the followers to shift methodically from materialistic attachment to a spiritual life. While it includes a spiritual component, the early stages focus more on learning and leading a prosperous materialistic life. The later stages focus more on detaching oneself from a materialistic life and following a spiritual path that leads to the final stage of full absorption in the spiritual quest.

Gods and goddesses that the Hindus worship in their daily lives depict the different aspects of the Supreme Soul. Many Hindus believe in the grace of the gods or goddesses to lead them to inner peace and *moksha.*

Although most Hindus do, the faith does not require one to worship a god or a goddess, or even subscribe to the concept of gods or goddesses. Instead, the believers can follow a path of meditation, stop the vagaries of mind, achieve inner peace, and attain *moksha.* Like a bird flying from point A to point B, Hinduism focuses on getting to point B—connecting with the Supreme Soul—rather than the path taken to get to point B.

To suit the person's devotional, emotional, and cerebral makeup, Hinduism shows the different paths to the Supreme Soul but does not dictate any of them. Actually, it says that there may be many other equally good or even better paths to *moksha.*

Most of the sacred scriptures of the Hindus appear to be spiritual and contemplative. Many consider the Bhagavad Gita, commonly known as the Gita, as the scripture that comes closest to representing the essence of Hinduism.

Hinduism, a faith deeply cherished by nearly a billion people on this planet, does not try to convert or proselytize anyone to its faith. It generally has a tradition of respecting other faiths and advocating the concept of "live and let live."

2

EARLY YEARS

Only the creator knows when it created the world.

—Hindu mantra

$\mathcal{H}$induism is one of the oldest faiths in the world. Its roots go back more than five thousand years, and this is the only major faith that has been in continuous practice for all these years. As a part of their daily prayer, even today Hindus recite nearly four-thousand-year-old hymns.

Because Hinduism is not based on the revelation from the God in the heavens to a mortal on Earth, it is open to new spiritual truths and realizations.

Hinduism does not compel anyone to follow its faith or force its followers to abide by a particular form of worship. Being an individualistic faith, it is up to each person to decide how he or she wants to address and approach the Supreme.

Although Hinduism's holy books refer to the Supreme as Brahman, Hindus in their daily lives normally address the Supreme by different names such as Brahmatma, Paramatma, Parameshwara, Paramshiva, Parabrahma, Purusottama, Rama, Krishna, Shiva, Shakti, or just *Om tat sat.*[2] To make it easy for the readers, wherever appropriate, I address the Supreme as the Supreme Soul.

Hindus believe in working for their own liberation of the soul, freeing themselves from this *sansaar* (also spelled *samsara*), "the world of a continuous cycle of life followed by death." Hinduism exhorts one to seek the "ultimate truth."

Instead of calling it "religion," Hindus prefer to call their belief system *dharma*, which has its roots in the Sanskrit word *dhri*, "to hold." There is no exact word in Western thinking to describe a Hindu's *dharma*. Its precise meaning depends on the context used. *Dharma* is a combination of the following:

- Moral discipline, duty, and ethics,
- A vehicle to keep or bind all in a harmonious order, and
- The essence.

The "moral discipline, duty, and ethics" part is not very different, for example, from Christianity's Ten Commandments—concepts such as honor your parents and do not steal—but it adds others such as the ability to differentiate right from wrong, being peaceful, having compassion, showing kindness to all creatures, and practicing physical and mental non-violence.

The "vehicle to keep or bind all in a harmonious order" component is similar to other religions. It includes studying scriptures, visiting the places of worship, and participating in rituals that bring the faithful together.

The "essence" part is probably one of the unique aspects of the *dharma*. It is what holds up the existence of a thing. It is the essence of a human being or the reason for existence. For the Hindus, it is their *dharma* to seek the enlightenment, work toward inner peace, and attain *moksha*.

Dharma does not automatically make one virtuous. It is merely a tool or a means. It is up to the person to use the tool effectively to subdue the ego, and to control the mind and the senses so that one can connect with the divine essence.

***

There are many dates on when this *dharma* started. Archaeologists have found traces of Hinduism in the ruins of ancient civilizations, commonly known as the Indus Valley civilization, of Mohenjodaro, Harappa, and the surrounding areas.[3] These areas are in modern-day India and Pakistan. Based on the areas they have excavated, archaeologists estimate the

Indus Valley civilization to be from around 3500 B.C. Records show that the Indus Valley civilization was fairly advanced with streets and a city built on rectangular grids, houses with baked-brick walls, a water system, and an elaborate system of bathing and drainage. It probably supported around forty thousand to fifty thousand people.

Archaeologists have discovered a soapstone seal featuring a male figure in a meditative Yoga position surrounded by animals in the ruins of the Indus Valley. Experts believe that the people worshipped the male figure, Shiva, also known as Pashupati—the lord of the animals—as early as 3500 B.C. Archaeologists also found terracotta female figures, which are believed to be that of a mother goddess. Some Indian historians contend that the people in the region worshipped these gods as far back as 12,000 to 6000 B.C.; however, currently there is no corroborating evidence to support this claim.

The Indus Valley was named after the Indus River, which was known as the Sindu River in earlier times. The historians believe that Persians, who were the next-door neighbors, could not pronounce "s"; they pronounced "s" as "h." Hence, anyone who lived across the Sindu River was a Hindu. Later, the area became known as Hindustan, "Hindu's place," or the land of the Hindus. Having changed their country's name to Iran or "the land of the Aryans" in the 1930s, Persians are called Iranians today.

For a long time, the word "Hindu" stood for a region and the people of that region. For example, centuries ago, Persians and Arabs called the Muslims from India "Hindavi" Muslims. To differentiate the Muslims and Christians in India from the outside world, many early British documents referred to them as "Hindoo" Muslims and "Hindoo" Christians.[4]

Even the current name of the country India came from the word "Hindu." The Greeks dropped the "h" and called the region "indoi," which the West later came to know as India.

***

Over the centuries, various migrating tribes settled in the Gangetic and Indus River plains because they were fertile lands with good weather. Based on the commonality between the Indo-European languages, western Indologists believe that the last major group to settle in masses was the proto-Indo-European group, who called themselves Aryans. Another faction of the same proto-Indo-Europeans settled in Europe.

Indology is an academic study of the languages, cultures, histories, and religions of the Indian subcontinent—the geographical region that includes the current nations of Pakistan, India, Bangladesh, Bhutan, Sri Lanka, and Nepal. "Indo-European" is a term coined to designate a family of languages with implied common ancestry. The European languages include Greek, Slavic, Celtic, Germanic including English, and Italic including Latin, French, and Spanish.

Even though there is no exact record, Western Indologists believe that the Aryans entered India from its western frontiers sometime around 3000 to 1500 B.C. with the major influx around 2000 B.C. They also believe that Aryans, being adept equestrians and charioteers, overwhelmed the locals; the incursion was a conquest. The word Aryan meant the "noble folks," until a German, Adolf Hitler, made calling oneself an Aryan a badge of shame.

Some of the Hindu gods appear to be similar to some of the gods worshipped by the Greeks, Romans, and Germans before the time of Christ. Scholars consider the Hindu sky god, Dyaus Pitr, to be the same as the Greek god Zeus, the Roman god Jupiter, or the German god Tiw; the Hindu god Varuna the same as the Greek god Ouranos; and the Hindu god Indra the same as the Norse god Thor.

Despite the hypothesis that the people who migrated to Europe and India came from the same proto-Indo-European branch, the belief systems that emerged in Europe differed greatly from the one that sprouted in the Indus Valley. While the belief that developed in the Indus Valley generally promoted harmony between humankind and God, the European beliefs contained a certain level of tension between God and man. According to Greek legends, the King of the Gods, Zeus, ordered the creation of a woman to punish humanity. Pandora, a "beautiful evil" with seductive gifts, was the first woman on Earth, a person responsible for bringing all the evils to humankind.

The tension between God and humankind is evident, for example, even in Christianity. Having defied God—by eating the forbidden fruit—Adam and Eve were punished, and humanity bears the sin for eternity. Eve, a woman created from the body of a man, Adam, was blamed for enticing the man and plunging humanity into everlasting sin. The concept of original sin is central to Christianity.

From Pandora to Eve, the belief system also appears to blame women for many of humanity's woes.

In addition to promoting harmony between the gods and humankind, goddesses are central to Hinduism. Gods and goddesses are two sides of the same coin.

Instead of calling them Aryans, Hindus refer to their ancestors as Aryas. Despite sounding similar, there is some debate on whether Aryas are the same as the Aryans. Some Indian scholars believe that any similarity with the gods whom the Greeks and others worshipped and any commonality with the European languages is a result of the exchange of ideas between the various groups trading with the Hindus over the centuries.

Around the sixth or seventh century B.C., a renowned Hindu scholar of the time, Panini, wrote his great grammar of the Sanskrit language.[5] In his writing, he mentions the Greek script, which indicates that there were some kind of contacts between the Hindus and the Greeks.[6]

The historians believe that Pythagoras, who is commonly known for his Pythagorean Theorem, came to India in the sixth century B.C. and studied the philosophy of the Hindus.[7] India and Europe had a flourishing trade by land and sea routes centuries before Alexander the Great came to the East in the fourth century B.C. Apparently, India even imported European "beautiful maidens" for its Indian version of the harem.[8]

By 300 B.C., Greece had formal diplomatic relations with India; Megasthenes was the Greek ambassador to Emperor Chandragupta Maurya's court. He wrote a four-volume account of his eight-year stay (306–298 B.C.) in India. Megasthenes' description became the earliest significant eyewitness account of India and an Indian emperor's court by a European.[9]

Although there are no written records, Indian scholars believe that the Hindus and the Greeks were in contact with each other for many centuries prior to the seventh century B.C. These scholars contend that Aryas were indigenous to the regions surrounding the Indus River.

Rather than the hypothesis of the Western Indologists, that a mass migration of Aryans overwhelmed the locals and was a de facto conquest over the locals, very likely there was a continuous migration of different groups into the area because of changing weather patterns. It is probable that there were occasional skirmishes between the old inhabitants and the newcomers.

Four thousand years ago, most people were nomadic in search of more arable lands such as the ones near the Indus River. It is possible that the migrating groups infused their beliefs into the local beliefs and traditions, which eventually became the foundations of Hinduism.

Actually, the term "Hinduism" is a British invention used to differentiate Hindus from people of other faiths during the British Raj (1858–1947). Many Hindus still call their faith Sanatana Dharma or eternal *dharma*. Some also refer to their *dharma* as Arya Dharma and their society as Arya Samaj (society).

***

The quest to find the answers to the ultimate truths, such as the answers to why we are here, what is our place in the universe, and what happens when we die, led generations of eminent sages, called *rishis*, to years of meditation and intense concentration.

The Vedas are the Hindus' first set of major religious texts. Veda, derived from the root *vid*, "knowledge," is the book of higher knowledge. It was the higher knowledge that the great *rishis* were able to discern by raising their life-spirit to the plane of universal spirit through years of deep meditation.[10]

The Vedic hymns were in Sanskrit, a branch of the Indo-European language spoken by the people at the time. As with Latin, Sanskrit is no longer in common use. Some Indian scholars assign the earliest Vedic hymns to 3000 B.C., others to 12,000 B.C. to 4000 B.C., but most believe they were finally compiled around 1500 B.C.[11]

One of the problems with the Hindus is that they do not seem to give much importance to keeping historical records. It may have to do with the prevailing mindset of the Hindus of the time. It appears they cared more for the soundness of doctrine than the date of its origin or the background of the author.

Lack of accurate recordkeeping sometimes makes it difficult to put historical events in sequence. Frequently, I find that the Western

Indologists date the same event or the publication of a Hindu epic or its holy books from a few to several centuries later than the dates assigned by their Indian counterparts.

Historians generally believe that the great *rishis* created the initial parts of the Vedas. The families of these *rishis* were responsible for keeping the parts of the Vedas alive by reciting them repeatedly and passing them down through the generations until a great *rishi*, Vyasa Krishna Dwaipayana, with the help of four other great *rishis*, Atri, Kanwa, Vasistha, and Vishwamitra, compiled them into a written form.

The Veda says, "The sages make their voices heard with hymns."[12] Having the Vedas as hymns made it easier for the families of the *rishis* to memorize and pass them down through the generations. It is normally easier to memorize songs or poems than lines and lines of text.

Because the Vedas are a collection of inspired wisdom, Hindus consider them sacred. Vedas are the foundations of Hinduism. Besides Sanatana Dharma and Arya Dharma, some Hindus refer to Hinduism as the Vedic Dharma.

In addition to incorporating the inspired wisdoms and inner experiences of the *rishis*, Vedas also captured the local beliefs prevalent in the region at the time. People could not understand the natural phenomena and had no means of predicting or controlling the forces of nature. They believed that a powerful deity controlled these natural forces. The Vedas incorporated these as the gods of rain, lightning, thunder, and so on. Rewards and punishments in this life and the next life were a result of the level of appeasement to the gods. They believed in heaven and hell—physical places where people would go after death.

Thinking the deities were just like them, people made offerings of things they used in their daily lives such as fruits, flowers, milk, butter, grains, and livestock. They practiced ritualized animal sacrifices to appease the gods and partook of the meat as *prasad*, "something that is imbued with the deity's grace." They justified ritualized animal killings by saying "killing in a sacrifice is not killing."[13]

***

There are four Vedas: Rig Veda, Sama Veda, Yajur Veda, and Atharva Veda.

The Rig Veda is the first book of the Vedas. It is a collection of inspired songs or hymns. Rig in Sanskrit means "praise."[14]

The Rig Veda is considered the oldest religious book in any Indo-European language.[15] It is a collection of 1,028 *suktas*, "hymns," and 10,600 verses in all, organized into ten *mandalas* or books. In Sanskrit, *mandalas* literally means "circles." Hindus often refer to the individual stanzas as *mantras* or *richas*.

The hymns are dedicated to deities such as the ruler of the heavens, god of cloud and rain, Indra; the god of fire, Agni; the omniscient god of the skies, Varuna; and nearly three dozen other gods and goddesses. As the leader of the Vedic gods, Indra is also the thunderbolt-wielding warrior king and heroic conqueror of Anaryas, "those against Aryas."

Varuna is the Vedic god of the skies whose eyes are the stars, and the custodian and enforcer of *rita*, "the universal law and order."[16] Varuna is also the Vedic god of water and the god concerned with the moral and social well-being of humans.

Because of the Vedic importance of sacrifice, Agni has a prominent role as the god of fire. As the fire sent the smoke from the *yagya* (also spelled as *yajna*), *homa* or *havan*, "oblations to the sacred fire in a ceremonial fire pit," upward to the gods, Hindus perceived Agni as the mediator Vedic god between the human and the divine worlds. Priests chant the Vedic *mantras* in honor of the deity or deities during the *homa*. Oblations typically include items, which the ancient Hindus considered symbols of prosperity and fertility, such as grains of rice (with and without the husk), barley, sesame seed, and *ghee*, "clarified butter." *Yagya* is an elaborate form of *homa; havan* is an alternative name for *homa*.

Nearly one-quarter of the Rig Vedic hymns are dedicated to Indra and about one-fifth to Agni.

The Rig Veda includes many other deities.[17] With the passage of time, while the importance of some of the principal deities such as Indra, Agni, and Varuna has declined, several others such as Vishnu, a Vedic solar god closely allied with Indra, and Rudra, the Vedic god of storms, have gained prominence.

Even after thousands of years, Hindus still recite the verses from the Rig Veda in their daily prayers. One of them is the Gayatri Mantra, which essentially says:

We meditate on the illuminating radiance of the Sun. May
the Sun's brilliance inspire us, stimulate our thoughts.[18]

***

The Rig Veda stands out among the four Vedas. Most of the hymns in
the Sama Veda and Yajur Veda are from the Rig Veda but rearranged
for ritualistic convenience. The Yajur Veda is a guidebook for the priests
conducting the Vedic sacrifices; the Sama Veda contains the melodies
and chants that the priests recite during the special sacrifices to Soma.

One of the difficulties with translating Vedic verses correctly is that
the meaning is context oriented; the same word can mean different
things in different contexts. For example, Soma can mean a god of de-
light and immortality, peace, and tranquility, and is often associated with
the Moon. He is also a god who activates speech, rules over the mind,
and bestows intellectual powers. Soma can also mean a plant yielding
intoxicating juice, which is presented to the gods as a part of ritual, and
served as a drink as the elixir of life.

The Atharva Veda has about one-sixth of its hymns that are common
with the Rig Veda; it also contains hymns speculating on the nature of
the universe and other cosmic matters not found in the other Vedas.

Although the Atharva Veda is the last of the Vedas, it captures the
customs and the practices of the pre-Vedic times. The Atharva Veda effectively preserves the traditions of the period dealing with spells, occult
formulas, and charms used in sorcery and healing. It gives an insight
into the thinking and the problems of ordinary lives of the people of
ancient times.

***

Each Veda consists of four parts: the Samhitas, the Brahmanas, the
Aranyakas, and the Upanishads. Sometimes the Aranyakas and the
Upanishads appear similar, as the topics covered are alike. The Samhitas,
"collection" of the hymns, are the original core of the Vedas.

Because the Samhitas did not blend easily in the conduct of rituals,
Hindus developed a set of prose called the Brahmanas, "critical reflection or rational contemplation" to help the priests with the sacrificial

rituals and the *mantra* recitations.[19] It also included commentaries on sacrifices made to the gods and the associated rewards. The priests became central in the conduct of these sacrificial rituals and *mantra* recitations to appease the gods.

Animal sacrifices included cattle and horses. Horse sacrifices or *aswa* (also spelled *asva*) *medhas,* were most important of the great royal ceremonies. It was often the cherished desire of every king of importance to perform at least one *aswa medha* during his reign. The elaborate ritual was believed to bring prosperity for the kingdom and its people while it enhanced the prestige of the king in the neighboring kingdoms.

Even though the Brahmanas covered the rituals for the householders, it did not fully cater to a segment of Hindu life that came after the householder phase. Thus began the nearly thousand years of introspection, which ended with the incorporation of the Aranyakas and the Upanishads in the Vedas and, in the process, radically altered Hinduism.

***

Hinduism divides the life into four *ashrams,* "phases," to get the faithful to shift methodically from a materialistic to a spiritual life.[20] The phases are not divided equally; it is up to each individual to define the duration of these phases.

The first phase is *bramahcharya,* "the unmarried phase," when the person is expected to focus mostly on learning. The second phase is *grihasthi,* "the householder." It is the married phase when one has a family during which one enjoys all the materialistic pleasures and the pleasures of the senses.

The next phase is *vanaprastha,* which means "going to the forest." At the time Hinduism developed, there were small settlements with domesticated animals and farms surrounded by forests. *Vanaprastha* meant detachment from the active life as a householder within the settlement, akin to the retirement phase today. Many left the village to settle literally inside the forest. While there is no explicit guidance, a preponderance of one's hair turning grey and an increasing number of wrinkles on the face are supposedly the signals to start easing into the retirement phase.

The last phase is *sanyas*, "a life of deep spiritual contemplation with total renunciation of materialistic attachments." This stage prepares one to die with utmost inner peace and to aim for *moksha*.

In the Vedic times, *sanyas* was the phase when people left on pilgrimages with little or no prospects of return. Often the arduous travel conditions made the pilgrimage challenging. For many, the cherished goal was to make it to the pilgrimage site such as Kaasi and die there on the shores of the Ganga River in peace. The Ganga River is called River Ganges in the West. Kaasi is known as Varanasi today; it is a city in northern India.

With the modern convenience of travel, pilgrimage is no longer challenging. People return from the pilgrimages and lead their life in their normal surroundings. Today, *sanyas* is more about renouncing the outer trappings of life and leading a life of deep spiritual contemplation.

***

Similar to the four phases, Hinduism defines four aspects of life: *dharma, artha, kama,* and *moksha.* These four aspects collectively are called *purusarthas,* "the goals of life." *Artha* is about pursuing and acquiring wealth, material possessions, and worldly success. *Kama* is about the pleasures of the senses.

Depending on the phase of life, the importance of those four aspects varies. While the *dharma* component is common throughout all the phases of life, one is expected to focus more on it as one gets to the later phases. *Artha* and *kama* play major roles in the second, the *grihasthi,* phase of life. Having enjoyed the materialistic pleasures from *artha,* and the sensual pleasures from *kama,* Hindus are expected to wean themselves slowly from this phase out to the *vanaprastha* phase.

Hinduism recognizes that when one fulfills one set of materialistic and sensual desires, new ones arise. The pursuit is never ending. The *vanaprastha* phase is the time for Hindus to work proactively toward controlling the desires and the materialistic attachments, subdue the ego, and start the process of liberating themselves from the cycles of rebirth, thereby culminating in the single-minded focus on *moksha* in the final *sanyas* stage.

In the *vanaprastha* phase, having relinquished the domestic life, Hindus could no longer perform the rituals and sacrifices as prescribed in the Brahmanas. Exploring alternative forms of worship for this phase of life led to the development of ideas that often contradicted the Brahmanas.

These ideas were compiled as the third part of the Vedas. Because of its association with *vanaprastha*, the "going to the forest" phase of life, these texts are called the Aranyakas, "wilderness or the forest texts." The Aranyakas opened the floodgate of spiritual quests for many centuries.

3

AGE OF ENLIGHTENMENT

Life is perennial search of truth.

—Yajur Veda

In Hinduism, the period between 1200 B.C. to around 200 B.C. was a time of great spiritual quest. Because it is not a faith based on the invincible word of God, Hinduism has no concept of sacrilege, heresy, or apostasy. Hence, no one feared impalement, decapitation, or public hanging for being a heretic and questioning the Vedas.

This thousand-year quest opened a new dimension in Hindu thinking and culminated in what the Hindus call *darshanas,* a word that stems from the verb *drs,* which means "to see." *Darshana* is a spiritual perception sustained by logical arguments and critical expositions.[21]

Over the centuries, the *darshanas* added new realizations of the spiritual truth on the foundation set by the Vedas. While some of the original Veda's Samhitas incorporated elements from the *darshanas,* some of the *darshanas* became the newer sections of the Vedas. Bhagavad Gita linked the original parts of the Vedas with their newer parts.

SPIRITUAL QUEST

Early Vedic religion was not radically different from other major religions of the time. Most of the religions worshipped a powerful god, typically a male, who was a paternalistic figure or an authority figure like a ruler. The god created everything in the universe and dispensed justice, rewarding those who obeyed his commands and punishing those who defied him. While people attributed good fortunes and great health to the god's blessings, they believed that the god's displeasure or wrath resulted in natural calamities and sickness. Some had more than one god with different powers, often with a hierarchy. There was good and evil; the good was the god, the evil was the anti-god or the devil. People tried to appease the god or the gods through ritualistic worship and sacrifice. Besides getting the obedient faithful to the heavens—a place of ultimate enjoyment and in some cases, a place of utmost materialistic pleasures that had eluded many faithful on Earth—the faith also served as the community's moral code of conduct.

Some of the *darshanas* that the Hindu thinkers developed over these thousand years were in the most part a radical departure from prevailing faiths of the time. Some even did away with the concept of good and evil or the god and the devil.

***

One of the *darshanas*, called Lokayata commonly known as Charvakas after the name of its founder, was too radical even for the Hindus of the time. Charvakas believed that there was no god or afterlife, and promoted maximum materialistic and sensual pleasures in one's lifetime.

Charvakas believed that people had no existence apart from the body and there was no life after death. They considered the physical body and consciousness to be identical. While denying the existence of the soul, they advocated that consciousness along with the physical body reverted to earth, water, fire, air, and space—the original components of all beings. They believed that this was the only world that existed; sense perception alone was the means of valid knowledge.

Charvakas advocated materialism and sensual indulgence. Hindus often cite the Sanskrit version of the following saying of the Charvakas:

As long as you live, live joyously. None can escape death.
When this body is cremated, how can it return?[22]

Contending that men invented the religions, Charvakas did not subscribe to any divine power and denied the authority of all scriptures. They believed that the religions made people submissive through fear and rituals, and the religious practices were futile activities promoted by self-serving priests.

However, the Charvakas' *darshana* did not have a lasting impression on the Hindu mindset and could not survive the test of time. Hindus do not consider it one of the prominent *darshanas*.

Despite the Hindus' rejection of the Charvakas' philosophy, one has to admire the audacity of these great thinkers for even advancing such philosophical skepticisms and religious indifferences, which must have been extremely radical for the time.

Unlike *mumuksus*, who desire *moksha* or *mukti*, Charvakas are called *bubhuksus*, who desire *bhukti*—worldly materialistic and sensual enjoyments. Hindus often refer to a Charvaka as a *nastika* or a non-believer, which is an antonym of *astika* or a believer in the Supreme.

Hindus regard the following six of the *darshanas* to be the prominent ones:

- Vaishesika
- Nyaya
- Purva Mimamsa
- Sankhya
- Upanishad
- Yoga

VAISHESIKA AND NYAYA

Vaishesika, founded by Kanada Rishi, states that fine particles are the basis of everything in the universe and God is the efficient cause.[23] God created the world, not from the start but by imposing order on pre-existing fine particles. Kanada Rishi perceived the fine particles as the basic building blocks similar to the subatomic particles of modern science.

Fine particles combine to form gross particles or the basic elements. Followers of Vaishesika believe that all material objects in the universe are made of the basic elements.

Incidentally, to identify someone as a *rishi*, Hindus normally add the word Rishi behind the name as in the case of the various great *rishis* who founded the *darshanas*.

Nyaya Sutra, founded by Gautama Rishi, resembles Vaishesika. Gautama Rishi encouraged Hindus to think and examine their faith in a more analytical and logical way. The Sutra has two elements: *adhyatma-vidya*, "metaphysics," and *tarka-sastra*, "logical analytical study." Listing a set of factors to consider in the process, Nyaya focused on a logical method to lead the mind to a sound conclusion and the attainment of highest good.

Both Nyaya and Vaishesika stated that knowledge led to everlasting good. Neither Nyaya nor Vaishesika subscribed to animal sacrifices and rituals. Both *darshanas* stressed logically examining oneself, nature, and the universe. Actions have consequences; good deeds lead to freeing of the soul from the body.

Even though Kanada Rishi and Gautama Rishi did not delve too deeply into the nature of the God, the *darshanas* perceive the God as omniscient, omnipotent, and responsible for setting the laws that govern the functioning of the universe and everything in it.

Academics believe that Vaishesika, being much older, could have influenced Nyaya, and Buddhism may have its roots in Vaishesika.[24]

PURVA MIMAMSA

Jaimini Rishi's Purva Mimamsa, which means "early critical inquiry," states that knowledge, as expounded by other *darshanas*, is not sufficient, and devotees must follow animal sacrifices and priestly rituals. It reaffirmed the importance of Vedic sacrifices and rituals and the exalted position of the priests.

Verse 10.90 of the Rig Veda, also commonly known as the Purusha Sukta, captures the Purva Mimamsa *darshana*. This hymn says that everything in this universe originates from Purusha. The Vedas describe Purusha's omniscience, omnipresence, and omnipotence to the ordinary folks by calling him a giant of a person with a thousand heads, a thousand eyes, and a thousand feet.

The Purusha Sukta says that everything originates from sacrifice. Just as, for example, Jesus Christ sacrificed himself on the cross for humanity's benefit, the entire Creation came into existence because of the sacrifice of Purusha's body. Just as Jesus went to live with his Father in the heavens after the Crucifixion, although Purusha was sacrificed, he was not destroyed for eternity. He was reborn. The Purusha Sukta says:

1. A thousand heads hath Purusha, a thousand eyes, a thousand feet.
On every side pervading earth, he fills a space ten fingers wide.
2. This Purusha is all that yet hath been and all that is to be
. . . .

13. The Moon was gendered from his mind, and from his eye the Sun had birth;
Indra and Agni [Rig Vedic god] from his mouth were born, and Vayu [Rig Vedic god] from his breath.
14. Forth from his navel came mid-air the sky was fashioned from his head
Earth from his feet and from his ear the regions. Thus, they formed the worlds.
15. Seven fencing-sticks had he, thrice seven layers of fuel were prepared,
When the Gods, offering sacrifice, bound, as their victim, Purusha.
16. Gods, sacrificing, sacrificed the victim these were the earliest holy ordinances.
The Mighty Ones attained the height of heaven, there where the Sidhyas, Gods of old, are dwelling.[25]

The last two verses focus on the virtues of the sacrifice and the rituals, their rewards, and the subsequent happiness in the heavens and thus capture the essence of the Purva Mimamsa.

Purva Mimamsa is also called the Karma Mimamsa or simply Mimamsa.

SANKHYA

Hindus credit Kapila Rishi for radically changing the Hindu thinking through his Sankhya (also spelled Samkhya) *darshana.* Scholars believe it to be the oldest of the six prominent *darshanas.*

Kapila Rishi's Purusha was very different from the Rig Vedic Purusha as discussed earlier under Purva Mimamsa. Sankhya did not perceive Purusha as the supreme god that created the universe and everything in it, including all the living beings on Earth. Even though the dictionary meaning of Purusha is "man," Kapila Rishi regarded the Purusha as the pure consciousness or the soul.

Sankhya saw Prakriti, which is distinct from Purusha, as the source of the universe and everything in it. While the dictionary meaning of Prakriti is "nature," Kapila Rishi viewed Prakriti as the source of the primal elements and the forces. Hindus view Sankhya as *dvaitya* or "dual," because it considers Purusha, the soul, and Prakriti, the universe, as distinct and separate.

Obviously, this Hindu definition of duality differs from its Western definition. In the West, normally duality connotes the difference between mind and body, whereas in Hinduism mind and body are perceived as one—both stem from Prakriti.

Sankhya concludes that Prakriti and its creation, the universe and everything in it including the humans, are *saguna,* "with *gunas,*" or having the varying combination of the following three essential *gunas,* "qualities":

- *Sattwa:*   State of equilibrium, in balance, free, calm, serene (also spelled *sattva*)

- *Rajas*:   The repulsive force, excitable energy, always active, restlessness
- *Tamas*:   Inertia, force of contraction, resistance, dense, dissolute

At the universal scale, when the *rajas* and *tamas* are balanced, Prakriti is in *sattwa*, "state of equilibrium" or "in balance." When in balance, the universe is still there inside the Prakriti but in a form called *kaarana*, "the casual state." At that instance, the Prakriti is unmanifested or *avyaktam*, which literally means "without vibration." The universe exists but only as potential in a manner similar to the potential energy of water in a river.

When the *rajas* and *tamas* go out of balance, all the latent energy is released, and that is the beginning of the Creation—the universe and eventually everything in it. The universe develops in phases; it goes through many steps until it changes to what it calls universal fine particles, which combine to become the gross particles or the basic elements. Everything in the universe is made of these gross particles.

Additionally, the mind and body, all the living creatures on Earth, and everything else in the universe, including the planets, stars, and the galaxies, are a result of this Creation and stem from Prakriti, and hence are connected. According to the Sankhya *darshana*, although Purusha, the soul, is constant, Prakriti is constantly changing. Time, space, and causation govern everything in Prakriti

Eventually when the *rajas* and *tamas* balance out, *sattwa* takes over and Prakriti reverts to the unmanifested or the undifferentiated state. The cycle goes on forever.

***

At the individual human level, Sankhya starts with universality of suffering, whether it is from the disorders of the body, the mind, or the external world. It believes that Prakriti is responsible for all the suffering including physical and mental ailments. Sankhya regards ignorance of the true self as the root cause of all the suffering.

Instead of recognizing Purusha as the true self, Sankhya says that out of ignorance one identifies with one's *ahamkara*, "I-maker" or the ego.

Just like the body, mind, and senses, the ego also stems from Prakriti. The main purpose in life is to recognize the true self; seek Purusha or the soul, which is eternally free; and to liberate from Prakriti's bondage.

Sankhya does not subscribe to the notion that one can liberate from Prakriti's bondage by the observance of Vedic rites, sacrifices, or rituals. One frees oneself from Prakriti's clutches by subduing the ego, balancing one's own individual *rajas* and *tamas*, and attaining a state of *sattwa* or inner serenity.

Sankhya advocates that once the soul is liberated from Prakriti's bondage it becomes omniscient and omnipresent. In Kapila Rishi's version, gods are souls that are free, and hence there will be as many gods as the number of liberated souls.

***

The hymn in Rig Veda 10.129 reflects the debate that had ensued during the Sankhya *darshana*. Some academics believe it to be an attack against the Sankhya *darshana*. This hymn, known as the Nasadiya Sukta, is possibly one of the earliest accounts of skeptical inquiry. It says:

> 1. THEN was not non-existent nor existent: there was no realm of air, no sky beyond it.
> What covered in, and where? and what gave shelter? Was water there, unfathomed depth of water?
> 2. Death was not then, nor was there aught immortal: no sign was there, the day's and night's divider.
> That One Thing, breathless, breathed by its own nature: apart from it was nothing whatsoever.
> 3. Darkness there was: at first concealed in darkness this All was indiscriminate chaos.
> All that existed then was void and formless: by the great power of Warmth was born that Unit.
> 4. Thereafter rose Desire in the beginning, Desire, the primal seed and germ of Spirit.
> Sages who searched with their heart's thought discovered the existent's kinship in the non-existent.

5. Transversely was their severing line extended: what was above it then, and what below it?

There were begetters, there were mighty forces, free action here and energy up yonder

6. Who verily knows and who can here declare it, whence it was born and whence comes this creation?

The Gods are later than this world's production. Who knows then whence it first came into being?

7. He, the first origin of this creation, whether he formed it all or did not form it,

Whose eye controls this world in highest heaven, he verily knows it, or perhaps he knows not.[26]

Reflecting the tenets of the Sankhya *darshana*, the hymn says the universe came from an unmanifested to a manifested state. In the unmanifested state, there was nothing whatsoever and the only thing that existed was the potential or "That One Thing." It was the *avyaktam* Prakriti, which existed without motion. Release of great forces and tremendous energy or "the great power of the Warmth" started the Creation.

As per the Sankhya philosophy, the gods were the liberated souls, and hence came later than the Creation or, as the hymn says, the "world's production." Hence, the gods could not know about the Creation.

The last two hymns above reflect the confusion created by the Purushas of the Sankhya *darshana*. Coming from the belief that everything originated from the great Vedic Purusha, these last two verses raised questions, which after centuries of critical expositions led to the advent of the Upanishad *darshana*.

UPANISHADS

Upanishad, which means "sitting by the side," captures the discussion between a teacher and students sitting side by side. Upanishad can also mean "to shatter" or "to wipe out ignorance." Even though the Upanishads are one element of the six prominent *darshanas*, Hindus recognized their importance and thus incorporated them into the Vedas. Upanishads are the fourth and the last part of the four-part Vedas.

Some refer to the Upanishads as Uttara Mimamsa, which means "latter critical inquiry" (c.f. Purva Mimamsa, "early critical inquiry"). Upanishads, being the last additions to the Vedas, are also called Vedanta or "the end of the Vedas."

While the Upanishads are generally accounted to be 108 in number, only a dozen or so of them are the most significant ones.[27] They range anywhere from a page to fifty pages in length. Some of the Upanishads have only eighteen verses of two or three lines.

Experts tend to associate an Upanishad with one of the four Vedas. Although open to debate, experts associate some of the prominent ones such as Aitareya and Kausitaki with the Rig Veda; Kena and Chandogya with the Sama Veda; Isa, Katha, Taittiriya, Svetasvatara, and Brihadaranyaka with the Yajur Veda; and Mandukya, Prashna, and Mundaka with the Atharva Veda.

Historians believe that the earliest Upanishads were in place by 900 B.C. Badarayana Rishi is credited for starting the Upanishadic *darshana*, which is similar to the Sankhya *darshana*, except that it believes all the liberated souls (Sankhya's Purushas) merge into the Supreme Soul, which it calls Brahman. The Upanishad *darshana* accepts Sankhya's Prakriti but it says Prakriti also stems from Brahman.

Brahman is the one, the Supreme Being, and the source of everything—all the individual souls and the universe. Brahman essentially represents the essence of the Purusha of the old Vedic text. Unlike Sankhya, the Upanishad is *advaitya* (also spelled *advaita*), "non-dual," and often referred to as Advaitya Vedanta (also spelled Advaita Vedanta)

***

Similar to the role of a catalyst in a chemical reaction, when a chemical reaction cannot proceed without the presence of the catalyst even though the catalyst does not actually participate in the chemical reaction, Brahman's presence is critical for Prakriti to create the universe, even though Brahman does not do any of the creating. Gita 9.10 says:[28]

I am the witness and through my witnessing Prakriti brings forth the whole creation, consisting of both animate and inanimate beings.

Similarly, when the soul enters the body of an individual, it does not react with the body, mind, or intellect. It is the catalyst or the witness that keeps one alive and enables one to exercise free will.

Because Brahman is above Prakriti, *gunas* that are intrinsic to everything under the realm of Prakriti do not affect Brahman. Hence, the Upanishads see Brahman as *nirguna*, "without *gunas*." In addition to being *nirguna*, Brahman is also *nirakara*, "without form, gender, or other physical characteristics." Hence, it is *nirakara-nirguna*. Therefore, instead of "he" or "she," Hindus refer to Brahman as "It" or "That."

Hindus describe Brahman as *sat*, "the ultimate truth"; *chit*, "consciousness"; and *ananda*, "eternal bliss." Unlike Prakriti, Brahman is not bound by time, space, and causation, and hence is unchanging and eternal.

Om (also sometimes spelled *Aum*) is Brahman's symbolic representation. *Om tat sat*, which means "*Om* that is the truth," is a common Hindu expression.

Hindus believe *Om* is the first sound that occurred when the universe was created. Hindus often start and conclude holy recitations with *Om*. The Mandukya Upanishad focuses on the sacred syllable *Om*, which it equates with the soul and Brahman.

Brahman is the source of *chit*. The living beings in the universe come alive because of *chit*.

The Upanishad advocates self-knowledge and trying through one's own efforts to realize the *sat*, the ultimate reality or the real thing, and attain *moksha*. Moreover, upon attaining *moksha*, a realm of *ananda* or eternal bliss pervades as one merges with Brahman.

***

According to the Upanishads, the mind, the senses, and the materialistic world, which come from Prakriti, create *maya*, "the veil of ignorance or illusion." The concept of *maya* can be confusing, especially when the discussion gets esoteric.

It simply means that what one perceives as real on Earth with the mind and the senses may not always be the universal reality.

For example, based on the observations from his senses, Sir Isaac Newton established his Law of Universal Gravitation. Although it helped explain the gravitational forces one encountered in one's daily life on Earth, Albert Einstein's Theory of General Relativity showed that Newton's Law did not truly capture the universal reality.

Based on one's senses, anyone can see that humans are different from animals, plants, and rocks. However, one has to go beyond the veil of the senses to understand the universal reality, as the ancient Hindu *rishis* did. They connected the humans, the animals, and the universe to the same primordial source and concluded that, in the universal context, all are made of the basic elements of the universe.

Based on real-life observations, one believes time to be absolute. As discussed later in the "Hinduism and Science" chapter of this book, by going beyond their senses the same *rishis* concluded that, in the universal context, time was not absolute, which Einstein confirmed nearly three thousand years later.

Similarly, when it comes to the spiritual self, in the universal context, *maya* creates a veil. *Maya's* veil gives one the illusion that one's true self is the *ahamkara*, "the ego." The veil makes one ignorant of who one truly is.

Maya's veil hides one's true spiritual self—the soul, which is the *sat*, *chit*, and *ananda*. Hindus speak of *maya* as "the illusion superimposed on the spiritual reality due to one's ignorance."

***

The Upanishads, which are the last parts of the Vedas, represent a radical break from their earlier parts. Rather than the rituals and the animal sacrifices, the Upanishads call on Hindus to follow a path based on knowledge and deep contemplation so that the individual's soul can join with Brahman. The Upanishads perceived the sacrifice of one's own ignorance, anger, malice, greed, and ego as a higher sacrifice than the animal sacrifices of the Vedic rituals.

In addition to being the last part of the Vedas, some of the Upanishadic concepts were also absorbed into other parts of the Vedas. Experts believe that the first and last books, *mandalas* 1 and 10 of Rig Veda Samhitas, are later additions, subsequent bookends around books 2–9.[29]

The crux of the Upanishads, the concept of the one Brahman, was also incorporated in the original Samhitas. The Rig Veda says:[30]

Ekam sat viprah bahudha vadanti.

It means, "Truth is one, wise call it by various names." These mere five Sanskrit words of the Rig Veda had a profound effect on the faith. It set the tone for Hinduism and made the faith uniquely different from other religions, which often claimed exclusivity and their God to be the only god.

"*Ekam sat viprah bahudha vadanti*" also allowed Hindus to see a form in the formless. Hindus no longer needed to wrestle with the dilemma, "How can I bow to It, who is formless, undifferentiated, blissful and in-destructible, who has through Itself and by Itself and in Itself filled up everything?"[31]

For example, they could perceive the formless and without attributes Brahman as Krishna in the Gita.

Krishna is the *saguna* god with all the human qualities. He is also *sakara*—one with the form, gender, and physical characteristics of a human.

Having the physical human attributes made it easier for the devotees to relate to and worship their *sakara-saguna* god Krishna.

The Gita is one of the most revered collections of spiritual wisdom in Hinduism.

***

Hindus consider the Brihadaranyaka Upanishad to be the oldest of the Upanishads. It is the longest and one of the most important Upanishads, and sets the stage for the resurgence of new thoughts in Hinduism.

Hindus regard the Brihadaranyaka Upanishad, which means the "Great Aranyaka Upanishad," as both an Aranyaka and an Upanishad. It is the point of transition between the two sections of the Vedas.

The Brihadaranyaka Upanishad captures the dialogs between a learned king and a legendary *rishi* in the presence of various other learned people, including some women.[32] Topics include the underlying nature of sacrifice, the formless and without attributes Brahman, and Brahman's relation with *atma, karma,* and *sansaar. Atma* or *jivatma* (also spelled *atman* or *jivatman*) is the individual soul, and *karma* is the consequence of every action and every thought. As mentioned earlier, *sansaar* is the world of a continuous cycle of life followed by death

In common with many traditions in the world, Hindus also have been searching for the *amrita,* "no-death or eternal life," or the nectar of immortality. Hindus often cite the Sanskrit version of the following three-thousand-year-old verse from the Brihadaranyaka Upanishad:

> Lead us from unreal to real; Lead us from darkness to light; Lead us from death to eternal life.[33]

Experts believe that the Chandogya Upanishad, the Upanishad of the singers of the Sama Veda compiled around the seventh century B.C., contains older material from centuries earlier. It has some common elements with the Brihadaranyaka Upanishad. The earlier Upanishads such as the Brihadaranyaka and Chandogya are in prose, while Upanishads of somewhat later composition such as Katha and Svetasvatara are in verse.[34]

The Chandogya Upanishad refers to Brahman as formless and without attributes. It says the soul is identical to Brahman and lies within every living being. Moreover, upon freeing itself from the clutches of the body, the soul becomes one with Brahman just as rivers become one with the ocean.

While most of the earlier Upanishads refer to the *nirakara-nirguna* Brahman, later Upanishads such as Isa and Svetasvatara refer to the *sakara-saguna* aspect of Brahman. Isa means *ishwara* or "God." The Isa Upanishad, which refers to Brahman as Isa, is also called the Isa-vasya (God-covered) Upanishad. With only eighteen verses, it is the shortest of the principal Upanishads. Speaking of the soul and Isa as one, the Upanishad says that for the enlightened one all that exists is nothing but the Self.

The Isa Upanishad describes the Self as unembodied, omniscient, beyond reproach, pure, and uncontaminated, and one who moves and yet does not move, who is far away but very near as well, and who although motionless is swifter than the mind.[35] The opening verse of the Upanishad says that one who is rich in the knowledge of the Self does not covet external power or possessions.

***

The Chandogya Upanishad is the original source of the most famous three words and the crux of Hinduism: *tat twam asi*.[36] "That Thou Art" is its literal translation. Some also call these words the Vedic *maha-vakya*, "Veda's great words."

Unlike English sentences with a subject-verb-object construction, Sanskrit uses a subject-object-verb or an object-subject-verb construction. Hence, the appropriate English translation of *tat twam asi* would be "Thou Art That" or to use the modern English it would be "You Are That." The individual soul is the same as the Brahman; thus, one is "That."

Various Upanishads capture the essence of *tat twam asi* in different words. For example, the Brihadaranyaka Upanishad says, "The Self is Brahman."[37] The Mundaka Upanishad says, "Know Him to be the Self."[38]

On the nature of the Self, the Katha Upanishad says:

> This Self is never born, nor does It die. It did not spring from anything, nor did anything spring from It. This Ancient One is unborn, eternal, everlasting. It is not slain even though the body is slain.[39]

The body is transient. One's true identity or the Self is the soul; in other words, one should realize, "I am the soul that has taken this body."

The aim of human existence is to free the soul. Capturing the discourse between a learned king and a great *rishi*, the Brihadaranyaka Upanishad describes in the following passage how attachments and unfulfilled desires will bring one back to this mortal world, and how attaining inner peace by freeing the mind from desires and attachments leads one to the immortal Brahman:

> According as one acts, so does one become. One becomes virtuous by virtuous action, bad by bad action.

> One revolves in accordance with one's desire, acts in ac-
> cordance with one's resolve, and turns out to be in accor-
> dance with one's *karma*. … After death, the soul goes to
> the next world, bearing in mind the subtle impressions
> of one's deeds. … Reaching the end … returns back to
> this world. … One who is freed from desires [and *karma*]
> … whose only desire is to know one's real Self goes to
> Brahman.[40]

***

Using a parable to illustrate the relationship between the body and the
soul, the Katha Upanishad says, "Know the *atma* or the soul as the rider
and the lord of the chariot, the body as the chariot, the *buddhi* as the one
who drives the chariot, the mind as the reins, the *indriyas* as the horses,
and the sense-objects as the road."[41] *Buddhi* is a combination of intellect,
wisdom, and discernment. *Indriyas* are the centers of sense perception.

The Katha Upanishad also says that the Creator has made the senses
outward-bound. For this reason, one normally perceives the external
world and not the inner soul. The wise ones, however, desiring immortality, realize the soul after drawing their senses away from the sense
objects.[42]

The Svetasvatara Upanishad says that God is pure consciousness and
pervades the entire universe. Although he is beyond space and time, he
exists within the human heart. He hides within all beings. He conceals
himself in all living beings, as a spider conceals itself in its web. He is
the witness and the guardian. The soul is the *antaryamin*, "the internal
controller."[43]

The Brihadaranyaka Upanishad adds, "The soul is the thread by
which this world [world of Prakriti] and the other world [Brahman] and
all things are tied together. … It [the soul] is present within the breath;
the breath, however, does not know it: the breath is its body; it controls
the breath from within. … It is present within the mind but is different
from the mind; the mind, however, does not know it: the mind is its
body, it controls the mind from within."[44]

***

The Upanishads attach great importance to the motive in conduct. They consider inner purity more important than outer conformity. In addition to saying do not steal, murder, covet, or hate, the Upanishads also say do not yield to anger, malice, and greed.

The Upanishads normally open and often end with their own distinctive peace chants. For example, the peace chant from the Katha Upanishad addresses the teacher and the taught:

> May the Supreme Being protect us both, teacher and taught.
> May the Supreme Being be pleased with us. May we acquire strength.
> May our study bring us illumination.
> May there be no enmity among us. *Om, Shanti, Shanti, Shanti.*[45]

The opening peace chant in the Isa Upanishad pays homage to the infinite aspect of the Supreme:

> *Om!* That (the Invisible-Absolute) is whole; whole is this (the visible phenomenal).
> From the Invisible Whole comes forth the visible whole.
> Though the visible whole has come out from the Invisible Whole, yet the Whole remains unaltered.
> *Om, Shanti, Shanti, Shanti.*[46]

Shanti means "peace."

Hinduism has many such peace chants. They often have messages of good wishes for humanity and universal peace. Hindus often start and/or end a religious ritual with a peace chant. Following is an example of a peace chant:

> May all be happy. May all be free from disease. May all realize what is good. May none be subject to misery.
> May the wicked become virtuous. May the virtuous attain tranquility. May the tranquil be free from bonds. May the freed make others free.

May all be free from dangers. May all realize what is good.
May all be actuated by noble thoughts. May all rejoice
everywhere.
May good betide all people. May all beings attain to their
welfare. May all the world be prosperous and happy.
Om, Shanti, Shanti, Shanti.[47]

YOGA

Yoga is one of the six *darshanas.* Although archaeologists and historians
believe that some form of Yoga was practiced in the Indus Valley region
as far back as 3500 B.C., Patanjali Rishi is credited with bringing a
structure to the old practice. Around 200 B.C., Patanjali Rishi wrote
the Yoga Sutra, which established a practical discipline of the body and
mind, leading to psychic and spiritual training.

Patanjali Rishi saw Yoga as the discipline for *chitta-vritti-nirodha* or the
"suppression of the fluctuations of mind." Yoga stops the vagaries of the
mind.

While the Sankhya and Upanishad *darshanas* promote self-knowledge through one's own efforts and meditation to remove the veil of ignorance that hides the true self or the soul and to attain *moksha,* Patanjali
Rishi developed a structured method of concentration and discipline of
body and mind to remove that veil. Patanjali Rishi advocated that only a
disciplined method of concentration can free the soul from the clutches
of the Prakriti—the matter, the senses, and the mind.

Even though the Yoga Sutra calls it Kriya Yoga, it is generally known
as Patanjali Rishi's Astanga Yoga. *Astanga* means "eight limbs"; the first
five are the *bahira anga,* "outer limbs," and the remaining three, namely
dharana, dhyana, and *samadhi,* are the *antar anga,* "inner limbs."

Following are the eight steps of Patanjali Rishi's Astanga Yoga, which
lead to *chitta-vritti-nirodha* and the realization of the soul:

1. *Yama:*   Inner restraint, not to hurt living
                beings

2. *Niyama:*   Self-discipline, internal control, calmness

3. *Asana:*   Posture, sitting

4. *Pranayama:*   Breathing techniques

5. *Pratyahara:* Control the senses, to shut out the outside world

6. *Dharana:*   Intense concentration on an object

7. *Dhyana:*   Meditation

8. *Samadhi:*   Final realization and attainment of *moksha*

Hindus normally refer to Patanjali Rishi's Astanga Yoga as the Raja Yoga, as discussed later in the "Paths to *Moksha*" chapter of this book.

Hinduism offers various ways or Yogas to quiet the mind, attain inner peace, and reach the soul. Yogas are an integral part of Hinduism. The difference between the various Yogas is in their approach. For example, Shabda Yoga focuses on words, and Mantra Yoga focuses on *mantra* recitations, with the belief that words or *mantras* have great powers to raise the level of consciousness.

GITA

Prompted by Hinduism's belief that the truth has many sides, which no one can fully express, Hindus saw unity in divergence.[48] Through the Bhagavad Gita (The Divine Song), the great *rishis* showed the spiritual thread that connected the Upanishads with their Vedic past.[49]

The Bhagavad Gita or simply the Gita is a part of the Mahabharata, one of the two Hindu *mahakavyas,* "great epics." Ramayana is the other Hindu *mahakavya.*

The Mahabharata is a story that values faithfulness, love and truth, victory of good over evil, and knowledge and wisdom over ignorance.

The background is a battlefield with two factions of the royal family getting ready to fight for the right to rule a kingdom. The central character in the Gita is Arjuna, a prince who is reluctant to fight the members of his close family. The Gita is the collection of the dialogs between Krishna, God, who came to Earth in a human form, and Arjuna, the prince, in a moral dilemma.

Symbology is intrinsic to Hinduism. The battle in the Gita represents the conflicting desires within everyone. One is not at peace with oneself until one realizes one's true self.

The Gita was composed in the fourth or fifth century B.C., with minor alterations over the centuries—possibly up to the second century A.D.[50]

In the Gita, the great *rishis* use the Krishna-Arjuna discourse to synthesize the Vedic Samhita's devotional approach with the Upanishad's deeply spiritual and knowledge-based *darshana* and Yoga's physical and mental disciplines.

***

Gita 17.23 says that Krishna is the embodiment of *Om tat sat,* or Brahman itself. The following passages from the Gita say that Krishna in reality is the same as the Purusha of Veda's Samhitas, and the various Vedic gods are the different forms of the same Supreme:

> With the mind disciplined by the practice of Yoga, thinking of nothing else, constantly engaged in contemplation of Me [Krishna], you will attain the supreme divine Purusha. (Gita 8.8)

> [Arjuna says to Krishna] You are the Purusha, the ultimate reality. You are the knower and the knowable, the supreme goal. It is You who pervades the universe, assuming endless forms. You are Vayu [Vedic wind god], Yama [Vedic god of death], Agni [Vedic god of fire], Varuna [Vedic omniscient god of the skies, enforcer of universal

law and order, and god of water], the Sasanka [Vedic
moon-god], Prajapati [predecessor to Vedic Purusha] ...
(Gita 11.38–39)

Ekam sat viprah bahudha vadanti allowed the Hindus to perceive
Krishna, Purusha, and the Vedic gods as Brahman. Through these
five words in Sanskrit, the Gita showed the Upanishadic link with its
Vedic past. The Gita in the following passages describes the Supreme
as the source of everything and expounds on its relationship with the
Upanishads' Prakriti:

> Know that all beings have evolved from this Prakriti, and
> that I am the source of the entire creation, and into Me,
> again it dissolves. (Gita 7.6)

> All creatures re-enter My Prakriti at the end of the world
> cycle [*kalpa*], and at the beginning of Creation, I send
> them forth again. (Gita 9.7)

> The entire universe deluded by the three *gunas* [of
> Prakriti namely, *sattwa*, *rajas* and *tamas*] fails to recognize
> Me—supreme, imperishable and above the *gunas*. (Gita
> 7.13)

Adopting the principles of the Upanishads, the Gita shows how the
individual soul is the same as the Supreme Soul. It speaks of the soul as
eternal and everlasting. The Gita also describes the relationship the soul
has with the mind, the senses, and the physical body. It also addresses
what happens to the soul after the body dies:

> The Soul dwelling in the body is really the same as
> the Supreme, who is the Witness, the true Guide, the
> Sustainer of all, the Experiencer [as the embodied soul],
> the Great Lord and the Supreme Soul. (Gita 13.22)

> The soul is never born nor dies; nor does it become only
> after being born. For it is unborn, eternal, permanent

and primeval … omnipresent, immovable, eternal. (Gita
2.20, 2.24)

The soul in this body is a particle of My own being, which
draws round itself the mind, and the five senses, which
rest in Prakriti. (Gita 15.7)

Just as a man sheds worn-out garments and puts on other
new ones, likewise the embodied soul casts off worn-out
bodies and enters into others, which are new. (Gita 2.22)

Just as the wind carries the perfumes from their source,
so too the soul takes the fragrances [from the mind, *gunas*, and the senses] when it leaves, and migrates them to
the new body. (Gita 15.8)

According to Gita 6.45, to escape the cycle of rebirth and attain *moksha*, one has to strive diligently, perfecting oneself through many lives.
Gita 15.5 adds:

Those who are free from false pride and delusion, have
conquered the failings of attachment, who are devoted to
the Supreme, whose cravings have altogether ceased and
have overcome the dualities of pleasure and pain, reach
that supreme immortal state.

Speaking of worldly attachments, Gita 2.62–64 say:

While dwelling on sense-objects, a person develops attachment for them, from such attachment springs desire, and from unfulfilled desire comes anger. From
anger arises bewilderment and confusion. Bewilderment
and confusion leads to irrational thinking resulting in
loss of reason, and from loss of reason, one goes to complete ruin. However, while enjoying the various sense-
objects through the senses, the self-controlled person

with a disciplined mind and free from attachments and aversions, attains the calmness of mind.

Gita 2.55, 2.56, 2.57, and 2.60 say that the mind is turbulent by nature. However, the mind can become less turbulent by controlling all cravings, limiting attachments to materialistic objects, being impervious to pain and pleasure, and freeing oneself from passion, fear, and anger. The Gita adds:

> The unthinking person can have no peace; and how can there be happiness for one lacking peace of mind? ... One who abandons all desires and lives free from attachment, egoism and longings attains peace. ... Having attained it, one overcomes delusion. Being in peace even at the time of death, one attains the Supreme Soul's Bliss. (Gita 2.66, 2.71, 2.72)

> Having renounced the fruits, which their action yields, the wise possessing an equipoise mind, are freed from the shackles of rebirth, and attain the blissful supreme state. (Gita 2.51)

> One who has inner happiness, inner delight and radiates from within becomes one with the Supreme Soul, who is the very source of bliss that resides inside. (Gita 5.24)

Although the Gita synthesized the earlier parts of the Vedas with the Upanishads, it did not refrain from disapproving of some Vedic practices. Gita 2.42–44 are critical of the promised rewards of the Vedic rituals:

> Those who are full of worldly desires, look upon heaven as the supreme goal and are devoted to the flowery words of the Vedas, which recommend many rituals of various kinds for the attainment of pleasure and power with rebirth as their fruit, are unwise. Those deeply attached to pleasure and worldly power, whose minds are carried

away by such words [of Vedas], cannot attain the deep concentration needed to reach the Supreme.

Because it is difficult for an average devotee to relate to the *nirakara-nirguna* Brahman and hence, meditating on it can be more arduous, Gita 12.3 encourages the devotees to follow the devotional path to the *sakara-saguna* god as it leads to the same goal more easily and naturally. The Gita's prime focus is devotion to Krishna to attain *moksha* through *bhakti*, "devotion," or the Bhakti Yoga, "the devotional path."

Even though Bhakti Yoga seeks grace from the Supreme resembling the Vedas' devotional path, these paths differ in some of the finer details.

The Vedas' path is heavy on priestly rituals and material offerings to the gods. As the following passages show, the Gita's Bhakti Yoga is about concentrating the mind on the God and the divine grace that will give the devotee the inner peace, which will lead to *moksha*:

> Take shelter in Him alone with all your being. By His grace, you will attain supreme peace and the eternal abode. (Gita 18.62)

> For one who always and constantly thinks of Me with undivided mind, who is ever absorbed in Me, I am easily reached. (Gita 8.14)

> With their mind fixed in Me, and their lives surrendered to Me, enlightening one another and speaking of Me, My devotees ever remain contented and take delight in Me. To those who are constantly devoted and worship Me with love, I confer that Yoga of wisdom through which they come to Me. I grace them by destroying the darkness born of ignorance dwelling in their heart by shining the light of wisdom. (Gita 10.9–11)

In addition to Bhakti Yoga, as the following passages show, Gita 3.3 recognizes the Karma Yoga, "Path of Action," and the Sankhya Yoga, "Path of Knowledge" (Sankhya Yoga is commonly known today as Gyana Yoga, also spelled Jnana Yoga. *Gyana* means knowledge):

I established the Sankhya Yoga for the contemplative person and the Karma Yoga for the busy, action-oriented person.

The Gita expounds the value of knowledge over sacrifices and rituals:

On earth, there is no purifier as great as the spiritual knowledge [of the Self]; one who has attained purity of heart through a prolonged practice of Yoga automatically sees the light of Truth in one's self in course of time. (Gita 4.38)

Some refer to Bhakti Yoga, Karma Yoga, and Gyana Yoga as Bhakti Marga, Karma Marga, and Gyana Marga. *Marga* means "path."

The Gita also speaks of *atma-aupamya*, which in Sanskrit means "equality of others with oneself."[51] It is the concept of "not doing anything to others, which might cause you pain if it were done to you, and seek for others the happiness and pleasure you desire for yourself." *Atma-aupamya* is the foundation for compassion and *ahimsa*, "non-violence in words, deeds, and thoughts."

***

By threading the Upanishadic views with the established Vedic practices and beliefs, the Gita enriched Hinduism. It balanced the Upanishadic *gyana* with *karma* and *bhakti*.

The thoughts in the Gita are deep; every fresh reading reveals new facets of the truth. Hindus look upon the Gita as one of their greatest scriptures.

4

BIRTH OF MODERN HINDUISM

One who is exalted and achieves communion with God is like a drop in the ocean, and is not in a position to describe its extent.

–Japji

The Upanishads describe Brahman as the source from which all things come—the creator, that which sustains them—the preserver, and that into which they dissolve—the destroyer. The Maitrayani Upanishad identified Brahma, Vishnu, and Rudra as the *trimurti*, "the triad"—creator, preserver, and destroyer aspects of Brahman.[52] Shiva was later identified with Rudra as the destroyer aspect of the Supreme.

Hindus perceived Shakti as Brahman's energy.[53] She is the Mahadevi, "the great goddess."

Even during the pre-Vedic times, Hindus worshipped Shiva and Mahadevi. Shiva was the Pashupati—the lord of animals in the Yoga position, whose soapstone seals were discovered in the Indus Valley archaeological excavation; Mahadevi was the mother goddess in the terracotta figurines.

Besides capturing the various aspects of the ultimate truth, the Gita also firmly embedded in the Hindu mindset the laws of *karma* and rebirth, the concept of *moksha*, and the different paths to *moksha*.

Some scholars consider the period between 200 B.C. and A.D. 300 the age of renaissance for Hinduism, and an epic age when the two great classics of Hinduism, the Ramayana and the Mahabharata, received their final shape.[54]

Similar to the Mahabharata, the Ramayana is also a story that stresses faithfulness, love, truth, and good over evil. Just like Krishna of the Mahabharata, Rama, the god incarnate, is the central figure of the Ramayana.

Hindus recognize Krishna and Rama as the *avatars,* "incarnates," of Vishnu, the preserver aspect of the *trimurti.* They believe that whenever evil overwhelms goodness, *avatars* of the loving protector Vishnu will physically appear on Earth to restore *dharma.*

By the epic age, Hinduism had incorporated almost all the main features and characteristics with which we are familiar today. Some scholars believe that by A.D. 300, the Vedic sacrifice at the altar also had started to give way to temple and image worship, meditation, and pilgrimage.[55]

***

With the core principles of Hinduism being fully set in the epic age, the focus shifted to the addition of commentaries to previous works and clarification of some of the esoteric practices. Hindus credit Shankaracharya for revitalizing Vedanta by advancing the tenets of Advaitya Vedanta in the eighth century A.D.

The Brahma Sutra (also called the Vedanta Sutra), composed between 200 B.C. and A.D. 400 by the Vedanta experts possibly for other experts, required expanded commentaries to help the ordinary folks understand it. Additionally, although all the Upanishads had the same core message, because they were works of different *rishis* over centuries, they lacked consistency and order.

Shankaracharya's commentaries on the Upanishads, the Brahma Sutra, and the Gita logically connected all the loose ends. The commentaries deal with the real nature of the Supreme Soul: how to get to it and what happens when one attains the Supreme Soul.

Shankaracharya advocated the path of knowledge and meditation to attain the Supreme Soul. He perceived the gods as the manifestation of Brahman to the human mind under the influence of *maya.*

Hindus refer to Shankaracharya as Adi Shankaracharya to distinguish him from other teachers, also called Shankaracharya, who succeeded him in the lineage he founded.

***

Although the highly metaphysical Vedanta captivated the intellectuals, it did not attract the overwhelming majority. They craved a path that appealed to their hearts and had more of an emotional content. They preferred the Bhakti Marga, the path that brought them emotionally close to their chosen god.

The *bhakti* movement led to the construction of new temples and the proliferation of temple worship. Over the centuries, mystics and poets such as the Alvars and the Nayanmars, and thinkers and scholars such as the Acharyas, who were mostly from South India, fueled the rise of various *bhakti* movements.[56]

Around the seventh century A.D., the Alvars had composed the Divya Prabandha, a collection of four thousand verses, which they sang in sacred shrines in praise of Narayana (another name for Vishnu), whereas the Nayanmars sang the songs from Tevaram in honor of Shiva.

Through successive generations, Acharyas attempted to reconcile the *bhakti* with *karma* and *gyana*. They revived the Pancharata, a devotional text devoted to Vishnu by his various names. Scholars believe that the Pancharata had its origins in the fourth to fifth century B.C.

Building on the foundations laid by the Acharyas, in the eleventh century, Ramanuja gave a philosophical justification for the *bhakti* movement. He disagreed with Shankaracharya's interpretations of the Upanishads, the Brahma Sutra, and the Gita—the three foundations or the *prasthana-traya* of Advaitya Vedanta. Using the same *prasthana-traya*, Ramanuja set out to give a theistic interpretation.[57]

Ramanuja called his philosophy Vishishta Advaitya, "qualified nondual," to differentiate it from Shankaracharya's Advaitya Vedanta. He advocated superiority of the Bhakti Marga over the Gyana Marga. Vallabha, Chaitanya, and Mirabai are some of the other great proponents of the *bhakti* movement within Hinduism. Hare Krishna movement has its roots in the traditions established by Chaitanya.[58]

Even today, Mirabai's *bhajans*, "devotional songs," which number anywhere from two hundred to thirteen hundred, have a wide and continuing appeal among the Hindus. Mirabai, who popularized Krishna worship in the sixteenth century, was a Rajput princess. She was a celebrated poet and a popular mystical singer. Regarded as a saint, she preached non-sectarianism. She was against gender differences and advocated mixing of the castes by keeping company with people from different castes. She deeply loved Krishna and dedicated her life to him.

Even within the *bhakti* movement, finer philosophical differences surfaced. While agreeing with Ramanuja and others on the superiority of the Bhakti Marga over the Gyana Marga, Madhava advocated the Dvaitya Vedanta (also spelled Dvaita Vedanta), a *bhakti* philosophy that differed from Ramanuja's Vishishta Advaitya. Instead of *tat twam asi*, Madhava saw it as *a tattwa masi* or "You are not That."[59]

Madhava believed that Vishnu, entirely by his grace, saved those who lived pure and moral lives. Evil souls were predestined to eternal damnation. He saw the Vedic wind god Vayu as Vishnu's son and his agent in this world. The distinction between the God and the soul, the concept of eternal damnation, and status of Vayu resemble aspects of Christianity. Scholars believe that the Syrian Christians, who were active in the region, may have influenced Madhava.[60]

Shankaracharya's Advaitya Vedanta views *atma* and Brahman as identical, but Ramanuja's Vishishta Advaitya sees *atma* as a distinct mode of an all-powerful God but not identical. Madhava's DvaityaVedanta sees *atma* as completely and eternally distinct from God. However, both Vishishta Advaitya and DvaityaVedanta rely on *bhakti* and God's grace for *mukti*. *Gyana*, "knowledge," leads to *moksha* or *mukti* in Advaitya Vedanta.

***

Bhaktas, the followers of Bhakti Marga, develop an intense emotional relationship and spiritual love for God through worship and prayers, and seek God's grace in self-realization of the ultimate inner peace and in attaining *moksha*.

Vaishnavism, Shaivism, and Shaktism are the three major *bhakti* schools. Followers of Vaishnavism regard Vishnu and his *avatars*, Rama and Krishna, as the personification of Brahman. Krishna, as a child, is endearing but mischievous. He grows up in a community of cow herders to be the *murali manohar*, "the handsome one with a flute," whom the beautiful *gopinis*, "dairymaids," deeply love.[61]

Around the first to second century B.C., the Svetasvartara Upanishad, while addressing the concept of *bhakti* and God's grace leading to *mukti*, introduced Shiva worship. It introduced devotion as an alternative path to meditation. Followers of Shaivism believe Shiva to be Brahman. They normally refer to Shiva as Maheswor, "the great God," and address the *trimurti* as Brahma-Vishnu-Maheswor.

Followers of Shaktism regard Shakti as the energy of Brahman; some *bhaktas* see her as the feminine aspect of Shiva. She appears as Mahadevi or in the various forms of the great goddess.

Even though the *bhaktas* regard their own God as the true personification of Brahman, they accept other's gods as the *ista devatas*, "related or friendly gods."

The *bhakti* movement received a big boost when external forces, which were alien to Hinduism, threatened the Indian subcontinent.

***

After Jesus' Crucifixion, the world of faith changed dramatically in the countries around the Mediterranean. Christianity started to take hold. After the destruction of their temple in A.D. 70, Jews began their exodus from Jerusalem. Some of the minority groups were subject to religious persecution. In addition to the people who wanted to spread their new faiths, Hindus were also seeing people coming to their lands to escape the religious violence.

Reportedly, St. Thomas the Apostle and his missionaries were the first Christians to migrate to India (ca. A.D. 52).[62] Jews started coming after the destruction of their temple in Jerusalem. Historians believe that the Christian migration accelerated significantly after the Council of Nicaea solidified the Christian beliefs. Historians believe that Arians—the followers of the Christian theologian Arius of Alexandria—who disagreed with the Council of Nicaea on some fundamental issues, migrated toward the East to escape persecution from their fellow Christians.[63]

By the middle of the seventh century A.D., the Caliphs with their army were busy spreading Islam with their swords. Islam replaced Zoroastrianism in Persia, a country on the western borders of the Hindu Indian subcontinent. Many Persians who wanted to retain their ancestral faith fled to the Gujarat region in Northwest India. In the nineteenth century, most of them moved from Gujarat to Bombay. Known as Parsis, they number around one hundred thousand and constitute the largest group of Zoroastrians in the world.[64]

Islam entered India through the Muslim Arab merchants in the seventh century, making it the last of the three Abrahamic religions to enter India. They settled mostly in western coastal regions.

Being a fertile land and on the sea route to China from the Arabian countries, the Indian subcontinent attracted hordes of invaders and migrants for centuries. For the last two millennia, it also has become a refuge for those fleeing religious persecution in their homeland. It did not hurt that for a long time India was rich with gold bullion and export surpluses.

However, unlike the previous groups who assimilated their beliefs with the locals, most of the newcomers had no desire to assimilate; on the contrary, they preferred to proselytize others to their faith.

***

Respecting the different points of view, when it comes to the Supreme Being or one's relationship with the Almighty, is intrinsic to the Hindus. Hindus respect personal choice and perceive other faiths as alternative paths leading to the same ultimate truth, and so as a rule, they do not feel a need to convert others to their faith.

For thousands of years, Hindus were accustomed to an inquiring approach to search for the truth. The following passages are examples of the discussion on the Supreme Being:

> Consciousness reflecting in consciousness shines as consciousness and exists as consciousness; yet, to one who is ignorant (though considering oneself as wise and

rational) there arises the notion that there has come into being and there exists something other than this consciousness. ... Consciousness is not created, nor does it perish; it is eternal and the world-appearance is superimposed on it, even as waves in the relation to the ocean.[65]

This universe is not real, nor is it unreal: it exists in consciousness, yet it does not exist (independently) in consciousness. Though appearing to be an addition to consciousness, it does not exceed consciousness.[66]

All indeed is Brahman; there is no world in reality.[67]

While these passages may be full of subtleties and are intellectually stimulating for some, they lacked the simplicity that appealed to the masses, which the proselytizing religions offered. By the eleventh century, among the Abrahamic faiths, the biggest proselytizing threat came from Islam backed by a new emerging political and military power.

For a faith to survive it has to connect emotionally with the masses. With the impending threats from the new proselytizing religions, the highly metaphysical discussions of Vedanta, which appealed mostly to the intellectuals, took a back seat. The *bhakti* movement offered a simpler, less complicated path for the average believers to show their devotion, affection, and fondness toward a lovable and adorable God and by his or her grace attain the *moksha*. Consequently, the *bhakti* movement gained greater prominence over the last millennium.

***

Even after centuries of exposure to the missionary religions and preaching of the exclusiveness of their faiths, average Hindus and the great Hindu saints and mystics continue to advocate that all paths lead to the same Supreme.

Ramakrishna Paramahamsa, who was a great saint in the nineteenth century and considered an *avatar* by his followers, was one of those who dedicated his life to preach the message of inclusiveness, unity, and the common bond between the faiths. Paramahamsa (also spelled

Paramhansa) is a title bestowed on those who have attained the supreme degree of spiritual perfection.

Ramakrishna Paramahamsa experimented with different paths, including Christianity and Islam, and concluded that one can follow any path whether it is Vaishnavism, Shaktism, or Shaivism or even Christianity or Islam if it helps in the realization of the Supreme Soul. The goal is to realize the Supreme.

After Ramakrishna Paramahamsa, his disciple, Swami Vivekananda, spread the message of religious coherence and unity. He advocated that all religions are the different paths to the same experience of the spiritual truth. Swami Vivekananda, a well-known Hindu seer of great eminence, revived the philosophy of Advaitya Vedanta.

In the late nineteenth century, Vivekananda presented Advaitya Vedanta as the core of Hinduism to the West. His teachings had great appeal.

5

RISE OF ORTHODOXY

Every man is the creature of the age in which he lives; very few are able to raise themselves above the ideas of the times.

—*Voltaire*

On A.D. 1206, Muslim rulers were finally successful in taking over large parts of the Indian subcontinent, primarily in the north. Eventually, from 1526 Muslims ruled almost the entire Indian subcontinent until East India Company, a British chartered trading company that had entered India in 1612, started to rule the country from 1757. The trading company transferred the power to the British Crown in 1858, and India became a part of the British Empire until 1947. Nepal is the only predominantly Hindu country in the Indian subcontinent not ruled by the Muslims, the British, or any other foreign power, and has remained independent throughout its known history.

Nevertheless, India is probably the only country in the world that did not fully convert to Islam despite the Muslims having ruled it for centuries. Today, nearly 30 percent of the population of the Indian subcontinent is Muslim.[68] The Southeast Asian countries known today as Malaysia and Indonesia, which practiced Hinduism for centuries, converted to Islam. Bali is the only region in Indonesia that retains its Hindu roots.

The Hindu, in the face of the clash of cultures and the external threat to its faith, fortified himself with conventions. Although the fortification might have saved Hinduism from extinction, it also gave rise to antiquated ideas and orthodoxy. A wife immolating herself (*sati*) voluntarily or under duress on the funeral pyre of her dead husband, enforced widow-hood, child marriages, polygamy, the dowry system, and the caste system with an added touch of untouchability became symbols of Hinduism.

***

With the arrival of the British, India became a hub for Western shipping, thus prompting more Indians to engage in global trade. Western medicine came to India. Indians got a taste of Western civilization.

Scholar and writer D. S. Sarma says, "The inrush of a totally different civilization put an end to all creative work for a time and an uncritical admiration for all things Western took possession of the mind of the educated classes coupled with contempt for things of native origin."[69]

The British also attracted a new influx of missionaries. Even though their life was devoted to spreading the word of Jesus to the natives, the missionaries were also educators who opened schools and colleges. While they taught Christianity as the only true religion, they imparted new secular Western knowledge in other areas. English became the com-mon language to connect linguistically disparate groups within India. Western education gave Indians the exposure to European cultures. Many Indians studied at the finest British institutions.

Western education also made people aware of the shortcomings in their society. In the nineteenth century, Hindu reformers started to advo-cate changes to the unhealthy practices that had seeped into Hinduism. For example, after eleven years of agitation against the practice of *sati*, Hindu reformers were able to convince the British rulers, who were gen-erally reluctant to interfere in the local religious traditions, to declare *sati* illegal in 1829.

Even though many Hindu women in the Indian subcontinent still struggle for their basic rights and the society in general continues to toler-ate violence and maltreatment against women, today, with the increasing literacy of women and their rising economic status, social customs such as enforced widowhood, child marriages, and polygamy are slowly disappear-ing. However, the dowry system with stories of bride burning or ill treat-ment of new brides for an insufficient dowry still makes the headlines.

In a society in which daughters are generally not entitled to any of the parental property, for centuries parents have given their daughters a dowry at the time of marriage as a parting gift.[70] The greed for money and materialistic goods, which has prompted some in the past few decades to exploit the system, is bringing the system disrepute. As long as the families perceive the marriage as a commercial venture, and the groom's family sees the new bride as a source of free money, the misuse of the dowry system is unlikely to abate unless the government imposes harsher penalties on the perpetrators.

***

The caste system continues to have a strong hold on the Hindu mindset. Some consider it Hinduism's Achilles heel.

Hindus trace the origins of the caste system to the Vedas. The following verses from the Rig Veda's Purusha Sukta speak of four groups:

> This Purusha is all that yet hath been and all that is to be; ...
> The Brahmin was his mouth, of both his arms was the Rajanya made.
> His thighs became the Vaisya; from his feet the Sudra was produced.[71]

The Brahmins focused on religious work, academia, and intellectual pursuits. While the priests are all Brahmins, not all Brahmins are priests; priests are just a subset of the Brahmins. By definition, because of their vocation, most of the teachers, the ancient seers, and the *rishis* were Brahmins. They were the architects of most of the *darshanas*, including the Upanishads. Even the ruler had to obey the Brahmin on religious matters.

Next was "Rajanya," the people who focused on the affairs of the state. Although referred to as Rajanya in the Vedas, today they are commonly known as the "Chetriyas" (also spelled Kshatriyas). Vaishyas, "merchants," was the third group; Sudras, "general laborers," was the fourth group. Gita 18.44 says:

> Farming, tending cattle, and trade are the natural duties
> of a Vaisya. Services of others are the natural duties of a
> Sudra.

Even though one could easily see that all the parts of the body are equally important, some have interpreted the Purusha Sukta to create an exalted position for the Brahmins because they emanated from Purusha's mouth and the lowest position for the Sudras because they came out of Purusha's feet.

The Sanskrit word for "caste" is *varna* or *jaati*. *Varna* also means "skin color." Believing that the indigenous people were darker than the invading Aryans, the Western Indologists, who perceive Aryas to be the same as the Aryans, believe that the Sudras were the subjugated indigenous people of non-Aryan origins.

The mere fact that Hindus worship Shiva and Mahadevi, the gods and goddesses worshipped by the indigenous people in 3000 B.C., prompts one to question the arguments made by the Western Indologists. Besides, not all the Aryans could have been just priests, warriors, or merchants.

Gita 18.41 says, "The duties of the Brahmins, the Kshatriyas, the Vaishyas, and the Sudras have been divided according to the qualities born of their nature."

It appears that for centuries, the grouping was fluid; people moved from one to the other. Based on one's capacity for knowledge and learning, character, and occupation, someone born of Sudra parents could become a Brahmin. According to the Mahabharata, "… it is not birth, not study, not learning, only the conduct that that makes one a Brahmin."[72] Even Buddha says, "Not by birth, but by his conduct alone, does a man become a low-caste or a Brahmin."[73]

Possibly, the grouping was ancient Hindus' way of recognizing the superiority of the spiritual and intellectual aspect of a person over his or her military skills, business acumen, and physical abilities.[74] Over the many centuries, the grouping evolved into the caste system.

Very likely, the caste system was a result of centuries of specialization, resulting in social stratification. By definition, the Brahmins were the custodians of the early Vedas. Because the Vedas had to be memorized and passed down for centuries until they were written down, and the sacrificial rituals were becoming more complicated, thus requiring greater skills to conduct them, it became a "generational" vocation. Rather than finding the best person to rule the country, a king preferred his son to be the next king. Similarly, the artisans passed their crafts down through their generations. The specialization started to become hereditary. The rigidity started to set in. The fluid grouping slowly morphed into a rigid caste system.

With the passage of time, the handling of refuse and excreta also became a hereditary occupation. Being outside the four castes, the group was an "outcaste" and was classified as the untouchable caste.[75] Mahatma Gandhi called them the Harijans, "the children of God," who today prefer to be called the *dalits*, "the oppressed."

***

Grouping is not unique to the Hindus. Societies have compartmentalized people for generations. Slavery, which created a subservient class, existed even before the time of Moses and continued to the last century in some countries.

In the fourth century B.C., Plato divided people into three classes: philosopher-rulers, warriors, and the masses. For centuries, Europeans maintained a clear demarcation between the nobles and the commoners.

In the West, for hundreds of years people accepted that they were born different, determined by God to be nobles or peasants.[76] Between the nobles at the top of society, and the peasants at the bottom, there were the merchants and the artisans. Supposedly, the nobles had the blue blood.

Professor of History of Religions at University of Chicago Wendy Doniger believes that the British, who were in India for nearly two hundred years and officially ruled the country for a century, raised the caste consciousness to a higher level by injecting the heavily entrenched British class system into the mix.

Professor Doniger says, "Whatever their social origins in Britain, the British generally joined the upper classes when they entered India. They saw the native princes, not the Brahmins, at the top of the multistory Hindu hierarchy and generally treated them as social equals. ... Thus assimilated to the class of some Hindus (the Rajas), the British tended to look upon their own people as members of a class so exalted above the

Indian rank and file that friendly association with them was taboo. They supported caste in many ways, both because they unconsciously tended to adopt the ideas of social stratification of the people they were ruling and because the Indian caste system echoed their own subtle and deeply entrenched social hierarchy."[77]

Some even blame the British rulers for their "divide and rule" policy of governance for keeping the caste system alive and, possibly, indirectly fostering it. The Hindu and Muslim factions and the caste divisions within Hindu society offered fertile grounds for the British to pit one faction against another.

***

Even though the British still maintain a subtle difference between the aristocrats and the commoners, as when a young prince marrying a commoner is considered a historic break with tradition, no one in 21st-century Europe thinks the nobles' blood is different from those of the peasants.[78] The shortage of labor because of the Black Death in Europe in the Middle Ages and the increased mobility of workers with the industrialization in later centuries may have helped diffuse the class segmentation in Western Europe.[79]

Even in India, the caste system would have disappeared if Hinduism had been a proselytizing religion. Starting someone from the bottom rungs as a new convert to handle refuse and excreta would have made proselytizing almost impossible.

In India and Nepal, the countries most associated with Hinduism, while most of the people identify themselves with a certain caste, today caste is no longer a barrier to people's professions. However, as a group the untouchables or the *dalits* seem still downtrodden because of their economic status.

Although Mahatma Gandhi said, "I regard untouchability as the greatest blot on Hinduism," some wonder if it is really a blot on Hinduism or just a social phenomenon masquerading as religion.[80] However, regardless of whether it is a religious or a social problem, just like slavery, the concept of "untouchables" is abominable and no longer defensible.

6

ELEMENTS

God is within us; we just need the eye to see it.

–Hindu saying

$\mathcal{L}$ike all great faiths of the world, Hinduism has three components. The first component deals with the scope of the faith, its basic principles, its ultimate goal, the way to attain that goal, and the holy books. The second component is mythology, which through legends, historical accounts, or supernatural beings attempts to validate the first component. The third component includes the rituals, festivals, ceremonies, pilgrimage, and worship, which appeal to the senses and make the faith attractive to the masses.

The festivals and the ceremonies help bind the believers together to form a common unit or units. Familial and social interactions, group activities, the colorful festivals, and the ceremonies help keep the faith front and center in people's lives.

DIFFERENT ASPECTS

"*Ekam sat viprah bahudha vadanti*" or "Truth is one, wise call it by various names," the five Upanishadic words in Sanskrit from the Rig Veda, allow Hindus to perceive the formless and without attributes Brahman the same as a god with a form and all its attributes.

Hinduism addresses the needs of men and women who are far apart in their intellectual and spiritual development. Its focus is on attaining *moksha*. For some, it may be by concentrating the mind on an object with no form or qualities, while for others it may be by the great devotion to the physical image of the god with whom they can relate in their daily lives.

***

As mentioned earlier, Brahma, Vishnu, and Shiva represent the creator, preserver, and destroyer aspects of Brahman in the physical form. Shakti, a female, represents Brahman's energy.

Actually, Hindus are not the only ones who perceive the different aspects of the Supreme. For example, Christians perceive the Holy Trinity—Jesus, the Father in the heavens, and the Holy Ghost—as the three distinct persons in one God. Jews have one God but, depending on what aspect of Yahweh they are referring to, call him by different names such as Elohim, Adonai, and El Shaddai. Muslims have ninety-nine names for Allah (for example, Ar-Rahmaan, Ar-Raheem, and Al-Malik) showing the different aspects such as compassionate, merciful, and powerful. It appears that people need to identify with the different aspects of God; it is just that different faiths decide to do it in different ways.

Generally, human beings are anthropomorphic. They like to ascribe human characteristics, attributes and form to nonhuman or supernatural things.

In Hinduism, each aspect has a *murti*, "sculpture," so that the devotees can relate to it lovingly. Because of the three aspects, Brahman is a *trimurti*; *tri* means "three."

Murti puja, worshipping the *murti*, is central to many Hindus, which most of them do at home and in a *mandir*, "temple." Although the *murtis* are reminders of the Supreme's aspects, Hinduism does not insist on *murti puja* nor does it condemn the practice. It is just a means to an end but not an end in itself.

In addition to the major gods—Brahma, Shiva, Vishnu and his *avatars*—Hindus accept many other minor gods and goddesses, which are in some ways associated with these major gods.

Besides showing devotion to the gods, Hindus also pray for wisdom. The Gayatri Mantra, which was mentioned earlier as the Vedic *mantra* Hindus have been reciting daily for centuries, is an example:

> We meditate on the illuminating radiance of the Sun. May the Sun's brilliance inspire us, stimulate our thoughts.[81]

The word *mantra* itself is a combination of two words, *manas*— "mind," and *trai*—"to free from." Hence, the purpose of *mantra* is to free oneself from the active mind and get to the inner core, which is quiet and peaceful.

Many of the *mantras* are from the Vedas. They are short passages that are continuously repeated to create inner peace and uplift spiritually. Most of the *mantras* are in praise of the Supreme or its many forms.

However, the *mantras* do not have to be connected to a god. Depending on the personal preference, people can choose a *saguna mantra* that refers to a god or a *nirguna mantra* that has no reference whatsoever to a god.

***

Brahma, Vishnu, and Shiva are *sakara-saguna*, human form with all the *gunas*. As the creator with all that energy, *rajas* dominates Brahma. Vishnu, being responsible for the power of existence and preservation, has *sattwa* as the dominant *guna*. *Tamas*, which is associated with the power of annihilation, dominates Shiva.

Brahma, Vishnu, and Shiva each functions through its own respective Shakti or energy, namely, Saraswati, Lakshmi, and Parvati. To make it easier for the devotees, Hindus show them as their consorts.

Brahma's consort is Saraswati, the goddess who is the epitome of universal intelligence, wisdom, creativity, learning, literature, arts, and music. She typically appears carrying a musical instrument. Vishnu's consort is Lakshmi (also spelled Laksmi or Laxmi), the goddess of wealth and prosperity. Seeing jewels on one of her hands and gold coins dropping from another of her hands makes it obvious to the devotee that she is the goddess of wealth and prosperity. Shiva's consort is Parvati (also called

Uma), who represents the gentler aspects of femininity, beauty, fidelity, and a dutiful loving wife.

Minor gods or demigods represent the other aspects of Brahman. Again, to make it easier for the devotees, Hindu legends speak of the minor gods as gods' offspring.

Ganesh, the god whom the Hindus typically worship first before worshipping the other gods, is the son of Shiva and Parvati. The family structure helps the average devotee see the link Ganesh has with Brahman.

Also revered as Vinayaka, the remover of obstacles in the universe, Ganesh is the god who clears obstacles from the path of *dharma*. He also helps clear obstacles from people's daily lives. Ganesh is potbellied, signifying the universe, and has the head of an elephant, which symbolically represents the physical ability to push obstacles away. Various myths and legends explain how Ganesh got the elephant head. As Ganapati, he is the leader of the demigods.

Hindus regard Ganesh to be the symbol of success, good living, peace, and wisdom. A small *bhakti* sect called Ganapatyas, "Ganapati worshippers," considers Ganesh to be the embodiment of Brahman equal to Brahma, Vishnu, and Shiva.

***

Faiths use symbols to convey the message to the masses. The dictionary defines a symbol as "something that represents something else by association, resemblance, or convention, especially a material object used to represent something invisible."[82]

For many, symbols have a more lasting impression on the psyche than written words. For example, Jesus on the cross is an iconic symbol of sacrifice for humanity. When Hinduism started nearly five thousand years ago, most Hindus were illiterate; thus, symbols conveyed a message they could understand.

Hindus show the qualities or the aspects of the Supreme that the particular god or goddess represents. For example, to show that Brahma, who is the creator of everything, is omnipresent, they show Brahma with four heads facing the four directions.

To depict the various qualities or aspects of the gods or the goddesses, they are shown with more than two hands, each holding a different object. The objects signify the various attributes. They will have as many hands as the number of attributes.

The god or goddess shown with only four hands and hence four attributes in a painting or on a sculpture inside one temple may have eight hands in another. It is a matter of how the devotees who built the temple or created the painting perceived their god or goddess at that particular time. Most of the time, at least one hand will hold an object to encourage the faithful to seek *moksha* or, through hand gestures, bless the devotee.

Abhaya mudra, "the gesture of fearlessness," is the *mudra*, "hand gesture," in which the palm of the deity is raised toward the devotee to inspire trust, dispel fear, and bless the devotee. Another hand gesture known as *varadan mudra* shows the palm of the hand turned toward the viewer and the fingers pointing down to show that the deity can grant the devotee's wishes.

Because showing gods with more than two hands is not common in religions such as Christianity, for example, this form of depiction in Hinduism can confound many in the West. For example, the icon of the Virgin Mary with three hands in the Troyan Monastery, about sixty miles northeast of Sofia, Bulgaria, may be the only unique icon in Christianity; her two hands cradle the infant Jesus, and the third hand represents the hand of God.[83]

Over the millennia, Hindus have used various animate or inanimate objects to convey the essence of their faith. The *padma* (lotus), a flower that has its origins at the bottom of a lake in the muck but comes up to the surface as a beautiful flower, carries a special significance to Hindus. They normally equate the lotus with humans stuck in the mud of worldly existence who can still reach enlightenment.

As a reflection of the high regard they have for the flower, Hindus even show the lotus sprouting from Vishnu's navel while he is sleeping. Hindus also depict gods and goddesses standing or seated on a lotus.

Hindus sometimes show the third eye in the middle of the forehead to represent someone who can see the past, present, and the future or the all-pervading eye of the Supreme Soul. To show that a god is eternal and everywhere, often they paint the god in the blue color of the sky. To accentuate the reverence for all living beings, each Hindu god has a companion animal or a bird.

Although there is no unanimity on the number or type of symbols associated with each deity or the meaning of the symbols, the following is an example of the symbols used and some of their commonly accepted interpretations:

Abhaya mudra
(blessing hand):   Hand gesture to bless the faithful on the right path seeking enlightenment; fear not

Ankusha (hook):   Remove obstacles from the path of *dharma*; the force by which all wrongful things are repelled

Blue skin color: Universality; color of the sky symbolizing eternal and infinite space

Book: Knowledge; Veda, the book of knowledge; knowledge of the ultimate *sat-chit-ananda* and *moksha*

Chakra (discus):   The Supreme Soul that brings multiple forms of the universe into being, similar to the spin of the *chakra*; ability to destroy evil

Circle of flame: Destruction and re-creation of the universe

Club: Power; ability to destroy evil

Coconut: Three dots represent the creator, preserver, and destroyer aspects of Brahman; represents purity, fertility, and blessing

Damaru (drum):   Rhythm of creation and dissolution; the sound at the beginning of the Creation

Elephant head: Power to remove obstacles

Flame: Flame that burns ignorance as the consciousness rises to realize the Supreme Soul; flame that burns the veil of *maya*; flame that

	destroys the world and helps create a new one
Gada (mace):	Force that will overwhelm
Padma (lotus):	Enlightenment
Potbelly:	The universe
Prayer beads:	Time
Sankha (conch shell):	Sound associated with the Creation of the universe similar to *Om*; symbol of victory over disorder
Snake:	Fertility; change of skin signifies a human discarding the old body and being reborn in a new body; shed the materialistic attachments just as the snake discards the skin; symbol of the destroyer aspect of Shiva
Spoon:	Offering made during worship
Swastika:	Good luck, wealth, normally associated with the goddess of wealth and prosperity, Lakshmi; an auspicious mark since ancient times (a Swastika with the ends pointing clockwise is considered auspicious)
Trisul (trident):	Represents the three aspects of Brahman; ability to destroy evil
Varadan mudra (grant wishes):	Hand gesture to show that God can grant the devotee's wishes
Water jug:	Source of life

BRAHMA

People who are new to Hinduism often get confused between Brahma, Brahman, and Brahmin. Brahma is the creator aspect—one of the three aspects of Brahman, the Supreme Being. As mentioned earlier, Brahmins represent the class of people that, for centuries, focused on religious work, academia, and intellectual pursuits.

Brahma is also known as Hiranyagarbha, "the golden womb"; Prajapati, "the lord of progeny"; Pitamah, "the patriarch"; and Viswakarma, "the architect of the universe." Brahma represents universal intelligence.

Interestingly, Hindus normally do not worship Brahma in their daily lives. In India, the land of temples, only a handful of temples are dedicated to Brahma. The Brahma temple located beside a sacred lake in the town of Puskar in Rajasthan is a major pilgrim center.

Hindus have many legends about why they do not worship Brahma as much as, for example, Vishnu or Shiva. Maybe the Hindus who seek liberation of the soul from Prakriti's entrapment may not care to worship Brahma, as he, through Prakriti, is the creator of the universe and, hence, the entrapment. Gita 8.18 says:

> All living beings emanate from the Unmanifest at the coming of the cosmic day; at the cosmic nightfall, they go back into the Unmanifest.

Through a simple formula, Hinduism says Brahma's day, or the twelve-hour cycle (*kalpa*), corresponds to 4.32 billion Earth years.[84] In accordance with this Gita passage, the living beings on Earth are created (*srishti*) at the beginning of Brahma's day, exist (s*thiti*) for 4.32 billion Earth years, and dissolve at the end of Brahma's day (*pralaya*). The living beings disappear during Brahma's twelve-hour night or 4.32 billion Earth years before the Brahma's *kalpa* or the *srishti-sthiti-pralaya* cycle starts all over again. The cycle repeats itself until the entire universe dissolves. Gita 9.7 says:

> During the Final Dissolution [*maha kalpa*], all beings enter My Prakriti, and at the beginning of [next] cycle, I emit them again.

Again, using a simple formula, Hindus believe the entire universe will dissolve (*maha kalpa*) in 311 trillion Earth years.[85]

VISHNU

Vishnu is the protector and preserver aspect of Brahman. Typically, he is shown with blue skin and with four arms, each holding an object reflecting the god's attributes, namely the *sankha, chakra, gada,* and *padma.* He wears a necklace with a rare gem, the Kaustubha.[86] As Narayana, Vishnu rests on the coils of Sesa Naag, a gigantic seven-headed cobra, afloat on an ocean. *Saligram,* a stone containing fossilized ammonite found mostly on the banks of the Kali Gandaki River in Nepal, is an aniconic representation of Vishnu.

Half-man/half-eagle Garuda is his animal companion and the vehicle he uses to fly around the universe. As Vishnu's wife standing next to him, normally Lakshmi is shown with only two hands but when she is shown as the goddess of wealth and prosperity then she has more than two hands, representing the various aspects of the goddess.

Hindu scriptures say that whenever evil overwhelms goodness, *avatars* of Vishnu will physically appear on Earth to restore *dharma.* For example, in Gita 4.7, Krishna says, "Whenever righteousness is on the decline and the unrighteousness is on the rise, I will reincarnate Myself." Krishna adds in Gita 4.8, "For the protection of the virtuous, for the destruction of the wicked, and for restoring *dharma,* I come into being from age to age."[87]

According to the religious texts, nine such *avatars* have already appeared in the form of a fish (Matsya), tortoise (Kurma), boar (Varaha), half-man/half-lion (Narasimha), and dwarf (Vamana), followed by full human form: Parasurama, Rama, Krishna, and Buddha.

Hindus recognize Buddha as a god on the same level as Rama and Krishna. When human wickedness gets unbearable, Hindus expect the tenth *avatar*, Kalki, to appear to destroy the wickedness from the hearts and minds, and to restore *dharma.*

Interestingly, despite all the religious stories behind the fish, tortoise, and others, the sequence seems to follow the scientific theories of evolution. Although several literatures list many more *avatars,* ten is the most commonly accepted number.

When Vishnu appears as an *avatar* such as Rama, Lakshmi appears as his consort Sita. Just as Lakshmi is Vishnu's Shakti or the energy of Brahman, Sita is Rama's Shakti.

Except when Vishnu physically appears on Earth as one of his *avatars* and Lakshmi appears as his consort, the gods and goddesses do not physically interact with the humans. It is as if the gods and goddesses are in a parallel universe or made of elements that do not directly interact with atomic matter.

Some Hindus even venerate *swamis* and saints as *avatars*. For example, many Gujaratis worship Swaminarayan, a *swami* prominent in the Indian state of Gujarat in the early nineteenth century A.D., as the god incarnate. *Swami*, "master or lord," is an honorific title bestowed on a guru of great wisdom. Some revere Ramakrishna Paramahamsa as the god incarnate.

***

Hindus worship Vishnu's *avatars* Rama and Krishna more than Vishnu himself. As mentioned earlier, Krishna, besides being the central figure of the Gita, is the *murali manohar*, "the handsome one with a flute," whom the beautiful dairymaids deeply love. The deep love is an illustration of devotion, a reflection of the passion that *bhaktas* have for their loving God and their desire for an intimate spiritual union. Hindus probably chant the names of Krishna and Rama more than the name of any other god.

Gita 8.6 says, "Thinking of whatever state one leaves the body at the time of death, that and that alone one attains, being ever absorbed in its thought." In Gita 8.5 Krishna says, "If one thinks of Me even at the time of death, one will come to Me."

Bhaktas believe that one will think of God at the time of death only if one is devoted to him or her previously also. Ramakrishna Paramahamsa says, "A man's rebirth is determined by what he has been thinking about just before death. Devotional practices are therefore very necessary. If, by constant practice, one's mind is freed from all worldly ideas, then the thought of God, which fills the mind in their place, will not leave it even at the time of death."[88]

Hindus often repeat the name of Rama during their final breath. Mahatma Gandhi remembered to say Rama as he was dying after being shot.

Hindus normally cover a dead body with a cloth with "Sita-Rama" printed on it. Mourners in many parts of India on the way to the cremation grounds normally chant *"Rama naam satya hai"*—"Rama's name is the truth." The chant is a reminder that Rama is the manifestation of Brahman, who is the *sat*, "the ultimate truth."

The holiest Hindu temples dedicated to Vishnu are in Badrinath, Puri, Tirupati, Trivandrum, and Dwarika.[89]

SHIVA

Shiva is the destroyer aspect of Brahman. Hindus believe that, as the destroyer, Shiva urges one to destroy the bond that binds one to the cycle of rebirths. As mentioned earlier, rather than referring to him as Shiva, devotees endearingly call him Maheswor or Mahadeva, 'the great god," and refer to the *trimurti* as Brahma-Vishnu-Maheswor. Shiva has many other names such as Rudra and Bhairava.

Hindus perceive Shiva in many forms. They see him in a meditative pose as the "Lord of the Yogas," sitting on Mount Kailasa in the Himalayas with a *trisul*, *damaru*, and a garland of *rudraksha* (rosaries of berries from a shrub of the same name). The Ganga River falls out of his matted hair. Because he drank a poison that threatened the future of the world, an act that obviously illustrates the compassionate side of his nature, Shiva has a blue spot on his throat. As an ascetic, he is smeared in ash with a garland of skulls, and has a laughing skull and a crescent moon on his head as ornaments. Snakes adorn Shiva around the neck, arms, wrist, and waist.

The crescent moon on Shiva's head, the garland of skulls, and the ash signify the impermanence of life. In addition to fertility and change, the snakes also represent death hiding around the corner. The skull on his head is laughing at people's inability to realize the transitory nature of life. The message is to meditate and work toward *moksha*.

Sometimes Shiva is in a Yogic position with the third vertical eye in the middle of his forehead. There are different interpretations on the third eye. Although some consider it the eye of the soul and its opening symbolizes the realization of the Supreme Soul through the mastery of Yoga, others believe that, as the destroyer, it is the representation of his latent *tejas*, "the fiery energy" that when opened will incinerate the universe in an instant.

Bhaktas, who worship Shiva as the personification of Brahman, see Brahma and Vishnu also in Shiva and as such show him with all the creator, preserver, and destroyer aspects as in Nataraja.

Shiva as Nataraja, "the Lord of the Dance," also represents Shakti, the energy of Brahman that animates the universe. Nataraja's dance is known as *tandava*. Nataraja as the cosmic dancer represents the dynamic universe where everything is always changing. Through the energy of the dance, all things, including the universe, come into existence and eventually disappear.

The Nataraja sculpture originated in South India around the tenth century A.D. It shows Nataraja with a peaceful and serene facial expression with the third eye; one of his left hands holds the flame that will destroy the world. Even though the fire signifies destruction, it also helps create a new world. One of his right hands plays a *damaru*, symbolizing the rhythm of creation and dissolution. The other right hand through *abhaya mudra* dispels fear, blesses the creation, and represents preservation, and the other left hand's *gaja-hasta mudra* points to his raised left foot, signifying that all those who approach him with devotion will find *moksha*. The right foot tramples a demon, signifying suppression of ignorance.[90]

Typical of most of the Shiva's *murtis*, Nataraja also has a crescent moon, a laughing skull on his head, and a snake wrapped around one of his right hands. He has flowing hair, which represents the Ganga River. A flaming aureole surrounds the whole image, indicating the cycle of creation and the destruction of the universe.

***

Bhaktas who regard Shiva as Brahman itself perceive Shakti as his feminine aspect. Shiva and Shakti are two complementary parts or the two sides of the same coin. If Shiva is the body, Shakti is the energy that brings the body alive. There is a common saying that without the energy of Shakti, Shiva is a *shava*, "corpse."

As mentioned earlier, Shakti appears as Parvati, who is Shiva's consort. To depict the complementary nature of Shiva and Shakti, Hindus have a male/female composite depiction of Shiva's right half from head to toe conjoined with Parvati's left half. Sometimes Shiva has a female earring on the left earlobe and a male earring on the right earlobe. Another very common symbol of the portrayal of the union is the Shivalinga—the union of Shiva's *linga*, "male sexual organ," with Parvati's *yoni*, "female sexual organ." Incidentally, archaeologists had found clay and stone artifacts resembling the Shivalinga in the Indus Valley excavations.

Sometimes lack of understanding of the essence behind the symbolism and taking the objects literally can lead to misunderstanding. For example, some Christians see Shivalinga as phallus worship, just as some Hindus find the Christian sacrament of partaking of the wafer and wine as the flesh and blood of Jesus as cannibalistic.

Most of the Shiva temples have Shivalingas; some temples show Shiva as Nataraja.[91] Shiva's animal companion is a bull, Nandi.

SHAKTI

In addition to the creator, preserver, and destroyer aspects of Brahman, Hindus also believe in Shakti, the energy aspect of Brahman. It is the feminine aspect, which sustains the universe. She appears as Mahadevi, "the great goddess."

As mentioned earlier, Hindus regard the consorts to Brahma, Vishnu, and Shiva, namely Saraswati, Lakshmi, and Parvati, as the various aspects of Shakti. Consistent with the famous five Upanishadic words in Sanskrit from the Rig Veda, "*Ekam sat viprah bahudha vadanti*," Hindus perceive Shakti in many forms. She is Ambika, the mother; Jagad Mata, the world mother; Lalitha, the smiling and auspicious goddess; and Lalitha Tripurasundari or Maha Tripurasundari, the beautiful goddess of all worlds. She is also the goddess of erotic love, Kameshawari; the auspicious Sridevi; and the queen of kings, Rajarajeswari.

As a loving wife, she is Parvati or the fair-complexioned Gauri, and as Uma, she nourishes the world. As Mahalakshmi, elephants flank her. She is Gaja Lakshmi when seated on the lotus while being showered with water from pots wielded by a pair of elephants. Farmers worship her as Annapurna, the benevolent goddess of plenty and harvest.

In her fierce form, Shakti is Durga and Kali. In the world of the good, the bad, and the ugly, devotees, besides looking for blessings, also look to the gods to destroy evil.

Moreover, it does not hurt to have a few fierce images to exhort the faithful to follow the right path. Unlike other major religions, Hinduism, being an individualistic faith, has no provisions for weekly sermons from the pulpit. For example, Christians have the option of creating vivid imagery through a "fire and brimstone sermon."[92]

***

Indologists believe that Shakti worship prevailed in pre-Vedic times. Possibly, the people worshipped her as the fierce mother goddess, who controlled the destructive forces of nature. In the Rig Veda, she is a *devi*, "goddess," such as Rudrani and Bhawani.

Bhaktas, who worship Shakti as Brahman, perceive the creator aspect of the Supreme in Saraswati, the preserver aspect in Lakshmi, and Durga or Kali as the destroyer aspect.[93]

Durga often rides a tiger or a lion and holds items such as a mace, trident, discus, conch, arrows, sword, and lotus. Hindu legends speak of gods creating Durga by combining their forces. *Bhaktas* show her with anywhere from four to twenty hands.

The "Purans" section of this chapter of the book briefly describes the legends behind how Durga protected humankind by defeating Mahisa, a fierce demon. Hindus have demons just as, for example, the Christians have their devil.

Although the legends describe the demons as frightening characters at times with non-human features, actually many of the demons are humans—often highly educated intellectuals who chose the path of evil. Gita 16.4 says:

> Hypocrisy, arrogance, pride, anger, sternness and igno-
> rance belong to the one born of demonic qualities.

Incidentally, Gita 16.2–3 also list the divine qualities:

Non-violence, truthfulness, absence of anger, renunciation, tranquility, aversion to fault finding, compassion for
all creatures, modesty, steadiness, forgiveness, patience,
and freedom from covetousness, malice and excessive
pride—these are the marks of the one born of divine
qualities.

As the goddess Kali, Shakti appears in forms that can be truly frightening. One of them shows her naked with her tongue hanging out and with a
garland of human skulls around her neck. On her left side, she brandishes
a sword in one hand while the other hand holds a freshly severed head with
dripping blood. However, on her right side, one hand shows the path to *moksha* and the other hand blesses the devotee in the *abhaya mudra.*

Hindu mythology speaks of Kali emerging from Durga's forehead
to kill fierce demons. In honor of killing powerful demonic giants such
as Chanda and Munda, she became Chamunda. According to the legends, her ability to drink blood stopped another demonic giant from
multiplying himself in battle whenever droplets of his spilled blood hit
the ground. Hindus endearingly also call her Mahakali, "the great Kali."

Bhaktas who believe in Vedic rituals and see animal sacrifice as a way
to appease gods sacrifice animals to Durga and Kali or their subordinate
devis (goddesses).

***

Goddess Kali's fearsome image has created many tales. During the time
of British rule in India, the media reported that a group of bandits called
Thuggees had created havoc by killing and robbing innocent travelers.

The British media of the time branded Thuggees as the Kali cult
bent on killing as a part of a religious ritual. Some wondered if the media had colluded with the missionaries to paint the faith of the natives
as barbaric.

Supposedly, the Thuggees surprised their victims and killed them by
tightening a scarf around the neck before robbing them. However, they
usually spared women and children.

Researchers have found that although many of the Thuggees did
worship Goddess Kali, it was not a Kali cult. These were highway robbers

creating mayhem. Checking the arrest records from the time of British rule, the researchers found that one-third of the Thuggees who were arrested at the time were actually Muslims, who obviously did not worship the Hindu goddess Kali.[94]

***

Hindu intellectuals have a different perspective on Kali. *Kaal* in Sanskrit means "time." These intellectuals believe that through the images of Goddess Kali, Hindus wanted to show the ravages and the destructive nature of time. The severed head, blood, and skulls represent the annihilation. Appearing naked, Goddess Kali reminds the faithful that time will kill them and that their attachments do not accompany them at death—they go naked.

Kaal also means "death." Just like the effects of time, Goddess Kali shows that no one can escape death, and she shows people the futility of greed and materialistic attachments.

The demons she kills are the demons of ignorance just as Nataraja tramples the demon of ignorance. Through her hand gestures, Goddess Kali directs the faithful to follow the *dharma* to seek spiritual enlightenment before incurring the ravages of time and death. She blesses the ones who have gained the knowledge of the transitory nature of life and are working toward their *moksha*.

HEAVEN AND HELL

Swarga Loka, whose literal translation is "the bright world," is the heavenly world or the heavens. Narga Loka is the hell. *Punya*, "meritorious deed or virtuous act," leads to the heavens, whereas *paap*, "demerit, sin, a wicked or an evil act," will lead to hell.

However, for centuries, Hindus have been debating about heaven and hell. Even though there are many stories in Hindu holy books about different layers of heaven and hell, some contend that heaven and hell may not actually be physical places in this universe or other universes. They may exist only in the mind.

> *Swarga,* "heaven," is that which delights the mind; *Narga,* "hell," is that which gives it pain. Vice is called hell; virtue is called heaven.[95]

> Desire, anger and greed—the triple gates of hell bring about the destruction of the soul. Therefore, one should abandon all these three. (Gita 16.21)

While the followers of formless and without attributes Brahman may be able to relate to the concept of heaven and hell in the mind, the followers of gods, aspects of Brahman with forms and attributes, perceive heaven and hell to be actual physical places.

Among those who believe in heaven and hell being actual physical places, some believe that they are within the creation of Prakriti, and could be in this universe or in a parallel universe. Being under Prakriti's creation, heavens and hells are also governed by time and space, and hence, are transient.

Some regard heavens and hells as transit points before rebirth. The Brihadaranyaka Upanishad says that after death, the soul goes to the next world, bearing in mind the subtle impressions of one's deeds.[96]

Bhaktas believe that those who are close to attaining *moksha,* akin to building a reservoir of good credit, can work toward *moksha* in heaven itself and then connect with the god of their devotion. However, others believe that one must return to Earth to work toward *moksha,* but they have a choice.

The aspirant has the choice to enjoy the peace and happiness in the heavens and use most of his or her good credits, and then return to Earth to start all over again. Alternatively, he or she can return to Earth immediately after a short transit in the heavens, and work on his or her *moksha* from where he or she left off.

Hells are places of pain and suffering. Resembling the options in heaven, the believers can exhaust their bad credits and suffer in hell, then return to Earth to start all over again. Alternatively, they can return to Earth as an animal immediately after a very short transit in hell. Because animals act mostly on instincts, the laws of *karma* do not affect them and as such, they go through many animal births before being reborn as a human.

Although inconsistent with most of Hinduism's holy books, in the nineteenth century, some intellectuals advanced the notion that humans, however evil, will not be reborn as animals. They believe that once one has reached human form, one will not revert to an animal form.

***

Some holy books list up to thirteen levels of heaven and hell, six layers of heaven with increasing levels of bliss above Earth and seven layers of hell with increasing levels of suffering below Earth.[97] Others believe in only three levels: heaven, Earth, and hell. Some believe that their ancestors live in Pitri Loka, "the world of ancestors."

Hindus also believe that the Supreme resides in the highest heaven, which they call different names such as Brahmaloka, "the world of Brahman"; Satya Loka, "the world of Truth"; and Baikuntha (also spelled Vaikuntha), "the abode of the gods," especially for the Vaishnavites. Hindus believe that the highest heavens such as the Brahmaloka, Satya Loka, and Baikuntha are outside the realm of Prakriti and outside time and space, hence are constant and everlasting.

With the grace of God, *bhaktas* hope to attain *moksha* and live in an eternally loving relationship with the god of their devotion in Baikuntha. Followers of the formless *sat, chit,* and *ananda* believe they will merge with Brahman in Brahmaloka.

These differing interpretations stem from the vast array of Hindu legends, myths, and holy books.

HOLY BOOKS

Indologists generally believe that the Hindu traditions have produced hundreds of thousands of texts in a wide variety of languages, most of which lie unstudied and effectively unknown. Written over centuries by different authors, these texts reflect the wide spectrum of spiritual realizations and philosophical discourses.

Hindus divide their vast array of holy books into two groups: *shruti* and *smriti*. *Shruti*, which literally means "heard," are what the great ancient *rishis* were able to hear by raising their consciousness to a higher level through years of deep meditation. Because the inspired wisdom of the great *rishis* reflected in the Vedas set the foundation of Hinduism, the Vedas are in a class by themselves. They are the only *shruti* texts.

All other holy books are in the *smriti* group. *Smriti*, which literally means "remembered," does not mean that these holy books are of lesser importance. For example, although the Gita is more popular than the Vedas and often people take their oath on the Gita just as, for example, Christians take an oath by placing their hand on the Holy Bible, the Gita is in the *smriti* group.

***

In addition to the Vedas, Hindus also have the Vedangas and the Upavedas, which are works that add to the wealth of knowledge, and the legends of the Purans. Hindus also have various *sutras*, "concise statements of principles or truths," and *sastras*, "authoritative treatises on specialized topics." Actually, *sutra* in Sanskrit means "a thread." Each *bhakti* sect has its set of holy books that provide guidance for the *bhaktas*.[98]

Despite being linked with the Vedas, most of the books are not *dharmic* texts. For example, the Upavedas are books of knowledge on secular topics.

Many Hindu books are not about the faith itself but depict the traditions, societal norms, and beliefs of the time. Some of the folklore that Hindus developed may have even influenced European folklore.

PURANS

Purans (also spelled Puranas), which mean "old" or "ancient traditions," include the legends and the myths of Hinduism. They include almost everything from the history of the universe, cosmology, and folklore to mythology. They appear to bolster the devotional aspects of the *bhakti* movement. Legends, folklore, and myths being more popular among the masses, the Purans are attractive to the common folks who may be less interested in esoteric discussions of the faith.

Although the Vedas are revered, most Hindus hardly ever read them; many Hindus may never even see one. The legends and the myths of the Purans are more popular than the Vedas or the passages of the Gita. Many of the prayers that Hindus recite in their daily *pujas* are not from the Vedas but are mostly the passages from the Purans.

Through the Purans, Hindus were able to thread pre-Vedic, Vedic, Upanishadic, and *bhakti* philosophies into captivating stories. This process also assimilated the various minor gods worshipped over the many centuries.

The Purans managed to link the demigods, or the minor gods responsible for the various aspects of natural phenomena, with an aspect of the *trimurti* and hence with Brahman. Through imaginative stories, the Purans capture almost every facet of Hinduism, including the animal sacrifices to Durga and Kali to the Yogas of the ascetic Shiva.

In the Purans, the Hindus divide time in phases or *yugas*, which means "the ages." The legends speak of four *yugas*: Satya, Treta, Dwapara, and Kali. The level of virtuosity, wisdom, and religiosity declines with *yuga*; it is at the highest in Satya Yuga and the lowest in Kali Yuga. Though spelled the same way in English, Kali in the *yugas* is different from the goddess Kali, and is pronounced differently.

The Satya Yuga is the Golden Age when *dharma* rules. There is no disease or hatred, and humans live for three hundred years. Things deteriorate with the passing *yugas*. In addition to the frequent devastation by floods and famines, in the Kali Yuga, malice, deception, and poverty reign. Incidentally, according to the legends, the Kali Yuga started in 3102 B.C., believed to be the year of the Mahabharata war, and will last for another 427,000 years.

Contrary to the imminent end-of-the-world prophesies from various sources in the West, using a story that an average Hindu can easily understand, the Puran explains that living beings will inhabit the Earth for 4.32 billion Earth years, before disappearing to reappear again 4.32 billion years later.[99] As mentioned earlier, the cycle of creation and dissolution continues in the universe until the entire universe dissolves in 311 trillion Earth years.[100]

The Purans speak of layers of heaven and hell. Possibly, to scare off miscreants from bad behavior, they include some gruesome accounts of hell.

***

Most of the major faiths have some versions of good and evil. In Hinduism, although everything in the universe is *saguna*, "with *gunas*," or having varing combinations of the three essential *gunas*, "qualities," namely *sattwa*, *rajas* and *tamas*, Hindus generally perceive gods as "good" and demons as "evil."

For example, Christianity calls the personification of evil the devil, and blames the devil for luring people away from the path of goodness and virtue. In Hinduism, even though the Purans speak of the demons' challenges to the gods, and the struggle between good and evil—the gods and demons, the devotees normally do not blame the demons for luring them away from the path of goodness and virtue.

Demons were the *asuras*. As per the Vedas, both the gods or in Sanskrit the *devas*, "the shining ones," and the *asuras*, "the children of darkness," originated from the same source—the god Prajapati, the forerunner of Purusha in the Rig Veda. With the passage of time, the *asuras* came to be seen as the opponents of God, and finally as the *danavs*, "demons," and the *rakhsasas*, "demons known for their extreme cruelty and for terrorizing humans."

One of the Puranic myths, the *samundra mathan*, "the churning of the ocean," speaks of how the gods and the *asuras* collaborated to find the *amrita* by churning a mythical ocean.

From the very beginning of time, it appears Hindus were searching for *amrita*, whose literal translation is "no-death." They believed that it was the nectar of immortality, which was hidden in the oceans.

The story details how they went about churning the ocean. While looking for the nectar of immortality, first they found *kaalakuta*, also known as *halahala*, a poison that threatened to wipe out everything. The probable moral of the story is to expect the unexpected.

Shiva nullified the poison by suspending it in his throat; swallowing it would have killed even the destroyer himself. This is the folklore behind Shiva's one of many names, Nilakantha, "the one with the blue throat."

Finally, when they got the *amrita*, both the gods and the *asuras* wanted it for themselves. According to one of the stories, through some trickery, the gods managed to get hold of the *amrita* and thus gained immortality. However, this started the eternal conflict between the gods and the *asuras*.

The concept of immortality prevalent in Vedic times took a different meaning with the Sankhya and Upanishadic *darshanas*. The "no-death" *amrita* became the "no re-birth, hence no-death" *moksha*.

Rather than seeking immortality through *amrita*, many Hindus today look for immortality through *moksha*.

***

There are eighteen *maha* (major) Purans, six each dedicated to Brahma, Vishnu, and Shiva, and eighteen *upa* (minor) Purans. Although the Hindus agree on the eighteen Maha Purans, there is no consensus on which ones qualify for the Upa Purans.[101]

The Markandeya Puran, Vishnu Puran, Bhagavata Puran, Garuda Puran, and Skanda Puran are some of the most popular Purans. Chandi, which the Hindus commonly recite, is a part of the Markandeya Puran. Similar to the story of Noah from Genesis in the Bible, the Bhagavata Puran includes the story of Manu, who saves humankind from a monumental flood.[102]

***

Chapters 81 through 93 of the Markandeya Puran contain the glorification of Mahadevi. Known as the Devi Mahatma, these thirteen chapters may possibly be the earliest and best-known Sanskrit text, consistently glorifying the Devi as the creator, preserver, and destroyer aspect of the Supreme. For the Shakti *bhaktas*, the Devi Mahatma is as important as the Gita to most Hindus.

The Devi Mahatma says that Mahisa, a shape-shifting demon that could change to anything at will, had ousted the gods from heaven. Having failed to defeat Mahisa, Vishnu and Shiva jointly requested Mahadevi to appear as Durga to kill the shape-shifting demon.

Fully armed by the gods with their weapons, Durga first tackled Mahisa's armies, and then confronted Mahisa himself, who changed forms during the battle. Durga killed the demon as he was in the process of changing to a buffalo, and hence the name Mahisa, "the buffalo."

The mythology of Devi Mahatma makes Mahadevi more important than the others, such as Vishnu and Shiva. Shakti *bhaktas* believe that someone who can even save the gods will be better than the other gods at saving the devotees.

Through the myths and legends, fables, and stories, which are intelligible to an average devotee, Purans enable the average devotee to appreciate the highest good. Purans bolster their inner spirit.

VEDANGAS

Considered supplementary to the Vedas, the Vedangas—the limbs of Veda—include any of the following six categories of texts designed to ensure correct performance of the Vedic rituals:

- Shiksa: The science of phonetics and phonetic analysis
- Vykarna: Grammar
- Nirukta: Etymological analysis, the study of the origin and historical development of a linguistic form
- Chhanda: Meter or prosody, the study of the measured arrangement of words in poetry or verse
- Jyotish: Astronomy, astrology, and mathematics; study of the movement of heavenly bodies for the auspicious timing for holy rites, as covered in the Jyotish Sastra
- Kalpa: Prescribe the correct performance of ceremonial rituals, as in the Kalpa Sutra, which include the following four Sutras:

  -   Shraut Sutra: Rules of Vedic ceremonies primarily for public rituals

- Sulba Sutra: Rules of construction and geometry, particularly the geometry of Vedic altars. In Sulba Sutra the legendary teacher and mathematician, Baudhayana, says that the square of the hypotenuse of a right-angled triangle equals the sum of the squares of the other two sides, which is commonly known in the West as the Pythagorean Theorem.[103] Historians believe Pythagoras spent considerable time in India. Physicist Stephen Hawking says, "Pythagoras probably did not discover ... the theorem that bears his name."[104]

- Dharma Sutra: Rituals, morals, and the social question of how people should conduct themselves

- Griha Sutra: Proper performance of domestic rituals, rites of passage

The Dharma Sastras further elaborate on the Dharma Sutra. Some of the contents of the Griha Sutra overlap the Dharma Sutra and the Dharma Sastras. As discussed later under the "Rituals" section of this chapter of the book, based on these Sastras and Sutras, Hindus have compiled a set of rites of passage that structure the entire life of the householder.

One of the prominent Dharma Sastras is Manava Dharma Sastra or Manusmriti, compiled around 200 B.C. to A.D. 100. It captures the ethical code of conduct, the social and moral order, and the way to perform the Vedic rituals. In addition to *acharya*, "the rules of conduct," the Sastra also addresses *pryaschittas*, "reparations for infringements of *dharma*," and *vyavahar*, "the civil and criminal law to administer justice."

Although some Hindu texts describe Manu as the progenitor of *manava*, "humankind," Manu actually may be a title bestowed on a person with great wisdom and devoted to virtue rather than the name of an individual.

Some of Manusmriti's observations show that human nature may not have changed appreciably in the last two thousand years. Speaking of desire, Manusmriti says:

> Desire is never satisfied by the enjoyment of the objects
> of desire; it grows more and more as does the fire to
> which fuel is added.[105]

Manusmriti in its twelve chapters covered almost every topic that people could possibly encounter in their daily lives at the time. While considered a treatise on the *dharma*, some of the topics such as the eight possible types of marriages may not be as relevant today as they were nearly two thousand years ago.

UPAVEDAS

Upavedas are the specialized books of knowledge. The Upavedas associated with the four Vedas are:

Rig Veda: Ayurveda is the Upaveda that deals with medical sciences and the science of life with guidance on an ideal and healthy way to live;

Sama Veda: Gandharvaveda is the Upaveda that deals
               with arts, music, singing, and dance;
Yajur Veda: Dhanurveda is the Upaveda of the sci-
               ence of warfare; it also addresses training
               warriors;
Atharva Veda: Sthapatya Veda is the Upaveda dealing with
               science, engineering, and architecture.

Possibly inspired by the Gandharvaveda, Bharatamuni developed his
Natya Sastra, which is a popular text among the Hindus engaged in the
artistic field. It shows the way to create eight different expressions and
the respective emotions.

Some contend that the legendary sage Bharatamuni's name itself
is attached to the Natya Sastra. They believe that Bha stands for *bhava*,
"expression"; Ra for *rasa*, "melody"; and Ta for *taal*, "rhythm." *Muni* is an
alternative name for a *rishi*.

Hindus have been using Ayurvedic medicine for thousands of
years. It perceives food as medicine; what one eats affects one's health,
well-being, and personality. Ayurveda lists foods that can ease ailments.

Ayurveda is getting increasing exposure in the West.

MISCELLANEOUS

Though not directly connected to any of the Vedas or the Purans, one
of the books the West is very familiar with is the Kama Sutra, the treatise
on love and sexual behavior.

Regardless of whether the Kama Sutra depicted the sexual adven-
tures of the privileged few with wives and concubines or was a purely
theoretical treatise of potential situations, scenarios, and not necessarily
the actual practice of the time, it definitely shocked the prudish British
rulers, who were used to the sexual norms of Victorian times. Although
people generally associate the Kama Sutra with sex, actually it also deals
with all the pleasures of the senses considered essential for a good life
such as music, art, good food, and perfume.

Hindus regard *kama* equally as important as one of the three other *purusarthas*, "the goals of life," the other three being *dharma*, *artha*, and *moksha*. Hence, the Kama Sutra, which is credited to Vatsyana, provides the sensual equivalent of the Dharma Sutra.

Not only do the Hindus have the Kama Sutra, but they also have a god of love, Kama Deva. He is the personification of sexual desire, portrayed as a youth wielding a bow with arrows. He shoots desire into the hearts of his victims. In the Puranic stories, Kama Deva is the son of Lakshmi and is married to an *apsara*, "seductress nymph," named Rati. Puranic myths are full of stories in which the gods send seductive *apsaras* to thwart potential threats.

***

One of the very prominent books, which may be relevant even today, is Artha Sastra, which covers governance, economics, the military, and affairs of state. Artha Sastra means Treatise on Polity.[106]

It has five thousand *sutras*, "concise statements of principles or truths," in Sanskrit credited to Kautilya, who was the chief minister to Emperor Chandragupta Maurya (reigned from 317 to 297 B.C.). Artha Sastra deals with seizing power through means fair or foul.

Kautilya argues that power can be acquired or enhanced by various *upayas*, "methods." These are *sama*, "appeasement"; *dama*, "gift or bribe"; *danda*, "punishment"; *bheda*, "planting dissent in the enemy's camp"; and *asana*, "sitting on the fence."

To these *upayas* of Kautilya, later generations added three other techniques: *maya*, "deceit"; *upeksha*, "remaining calm, taking no notice," or "ignoring"; and *indrajala*, "conjuring" or "trickery."

Maya used in the context of Artha Sastra is different from the *maya* discussed in the earlier chapters of this book as the illusion superimposed on the spiritual reality due to one's ignorance.

Not only the Hindu rulers but also, as the story in the Mahabharata illustrates, even the gods were not above using Kautilya's *upayas*. Even today, it appears many world leaders and politicians knowingly or unknowingly embrace many of Kautilya's *upayas* from the twenty-three-hundred-year-old Artha Sastra.

Even though some associate this Sastra with Hinduism, actually it has nothing to do with the *dharma*. The Sastra even advocates expediency to *dharmic* morality in managing the affairs of state.

The Artha Sastra says that political and religious authorities operate in separate spheres akin to the separation of the church and the state.

***

In addition to the *sastras*, Hindus have developed a collection of fables and folk wisdom. One of them is the Pancha Tantra. It consists of five volumes of stories written by a teacher to educate the princes on different aspects of governance. The Pancha Tantra is designed to confront a dilemma to make a moral and/or a political point.

The Pancha Tantra and its offshoot, the Hitopadesha, not only had a wide appeal in the Indian subcontinent but also were probably the most widely disseminated Hindu works throughout the world. The Hitopadesha says that hunger, sleep, fear, and sex are common to humans and animals; what distinguishes humans from animals is the knowledge of right and wrong.

Some believe that possibly as many as two hundred versions of the Pancha Tantra in fifty languages exist around the world. Indologists believe that the Pancha Tantra and the Hitopadesha influenced Middle Eastern and European story collections such as *Arabian Nights* and La Fontaine's *Fables*.

EPICS

The Mahabharata and the Ramayana are the most popular of all the texts in the *smriti* groups. These are the two Hindu epics written in *slokas* (also spelled *shlokas*). *Slokas* are hymns that rhyme.

The Mahabharata and the Ramayana exhort the faithful to follow a path of goodness and virtue, and uphold *dharma*. Hindus appear to have an insatiable appetite for the dramatic reproductions of these epics.

Because the people in many Southeast Asian countries practiced Hinduism until a few centuries ago, one can still see the Ramayana's influence in many of the ritualistic dances of the Southeast Asian countries.

MAHABHARATA

The epic story of the Mahabharata is set against the backdrop of a battle between two rival factions of a royal family: the descendants of King Bharata—the Pandavas and the Kauravas.

Upon the death of the Pandavas' father, the Kauravas' father became the new king. Interfamily rivalry ensued. To maintain peace within the families, the Pandavas were given their own kingdom to rule, which the Kaurava brothers resented. The Pandavas and the Kauravas ruled from their respective capitals, Indraprastha and Hastinapur, places which are north of the current city of New Delhi.

Yudhisthira, the embodiment of virtue, was the eldest of the five Pandava brothers. Arjuna, the central character in the conflict, is the third of the Pandava brothers.[107] Duryodhana, first cousin to Yudhisthira, headed the Kaurava brothers.

The Kauravas hatched a plan to banish the Pandavas from their kingdom by rigging a game of dice. Yudhisthira lost the game and, as a condition of the game, the Pandavas went into exile for thirteen years—twelve years in the wilderness and a year living incognito. The Kauravas usurped the Pandavas' kingdom and ruled over it as their own. Refusal to return the kingdom to the Pandavas after their return from exile led to the start of the battle.

While the story of the Pandavas and the Kauravas represents the conflict between two great forces with a common ancestry, it also depicts the battle of good over evil on the battleground of moral struggle—the forces that spring from the same inner source. Arjuna represents human conditions inside, torn between opposing forces of good and evil, right and wrong. The Mahabharata captures the basic tenets of the faith such as transmigration of souls, rebirth, *karma,* and *moksha.*

The Mahabharata, which the Hindus call the *mahakavya,* "the great epic," has a hundred thousand verses. It is, for example, fifteen times the combined length of the Old and the New Testaments of the Bible and seven times the combined length of the ancient Greek epic poems, the *Iliad* and the *Odyssey*. Historians believe that Vyasa Rishi, with help from his pupils, compiled the Mahabharata around the fifth century B.C. with changes introduced by later writers possibly until the second century A.D.

Vyasa was a *maharishi*, "great *rishi*," and is different from another great *rishi* with a similar name, who compiled the Vedas centuries earlier. Some scholars speculate that Vyasa may be a title bestowed on a great *rishi* rather than the name of an individual.

As a sign of ultimate respect, rather than calling them *rishis*, Hindus often address the architects of the Vedas, the *darshanas*, and the two great epics as *maharishis*.

Although writing in verses is much more difficult than writing in prose, the great writers of the major books in Hinduism such as the Veda's Samhitas, the Mahabharata, and the Ramayana wrote them in verse. Poems, songs, and verses are easier to remember or recite and are more pleasant to the senses.

The Gita, which is relatively small with about seven hundred verses, is an integral part of the Mahabharata.

***

Vyasa Rishi divided the Mahabharata into eighteen *parvas*, "occasions" or "events." The first *parva*, the Adi Parva, sets the stage for the epic. The second *parva*, the Sabha Parva, captures the gambling scene in the great assembly hall, which results in the Pandavas losing the game of dice and being banished in the wilderness for twelve years as captured in the third *parva*, the Aranyaka Parva. The fourth *parva*, the Virata Parva, captures the one year of living incognito.

The preparations for the battle start in the fifth *parva*, the Udyoga Parva. Coverage of the actual battle details is in *parvas* 6 through 11. The sixth *parva*, the Bhisma Parva, includes the Gita.

Peace is restored in the twelfth *parva*, the Shanti Parva, with the crowning of Yudhisthira. It is the longest of all the *parvas*. The wide-ranging and extensive discourse on ethics, *dharma*, and cos-mology starts in the twelfth *parva* and continues on to *parva* 13, the Anusasana Parva, which is the second longest of all the *parvas*. The fourteenth *parva*, the Ashwamedha Parva, deals with religious rituals of the period.

Death of some of the prominent figures such as the Kauravas' father Dhritarastra, who was born blind, is captured in the fifteenth *parva*, the Ashramavasika Parva. Besides being physically blind, Vyasa Rishi shows that King Dhritarastra was blinded by the love for his sons and refused to correct their *adharmic* ways. *Adharma* means "non-*dharmic*," acts that infringe on *dharma*.

Incidentally, because King Dhritarastra was blind, his consort, Queen Gandhari, voluntarily decided to blindfold herself for life. Although this was a sign of devotion of a dutiful wife, it also represented Queen Gandhari's refusal to see the *adharma*.

In the sixteenth *parva*, the Mausala Parva, Krishna allows himself to be killed in a hunting accident.

As the god incarnate, Krishna knew he was going to be killed and he let it happen. He had completed his earthly assignment and it was time for him to return to the heavens.

In Maha Prasthanika Parva, the seventeenth *parva*, the five Pandava brothers renounce the world and set out for the heavens. The last *parva*, Swargarohana Parva, captures the scenes in the heavens.

*****

In the context of the drama, Vyasa Rishi captures contradictory themes. For example, while it extols the virtues of marriage or having a wife, it also captures polyandry. Speaking of a wife, the Mahabharata says:

> A wife is half the man, his truest friend
> A loving wife is a perpetual spring
> Of virtue, pleasure, wealth; a faithful wife
> Is his best aid in seeking heavenly bliss;
> A sweetly speaking wife is a companion
> In solitude; a father in advice;
> A mother in all seasons of distress;
> A rest in passing through life's wilderness.[108]

Even though the Mahabharata includes polyandry, it is difficult to ascertain if it was an accepted practice of the time or merely Vyasa Rishi's figments of imagination to enrich the drama. Similar to Mother Mary being impregnated by the Holy Ghost in Christianity, the Mahabharata also captures conjugal union with the divine forces.

Through captivating stories, Vyasa Rishi shows the difference between *dharma* and *adharma*. He depicts the Pandavas as the embodiment of *dharma*, law and justice, and the Kauravas as the epitome of *adharma*.

Even though Hindus regard the Mahabharata as an *itihasa*, "history"—historical account of events that took place in 3102 B.C.—Mahatma Gandhi did not regard the Mahabharata as a historical work.[109] He says, "By ascribing to the chief actors superhuman or subhuman origins, the great Vyasa made short work of the history of kings and their peoples. The persons therein described may be historical but the author of the Mahabharata has used them merely to drive home his religious theme."[110] Scholars speculate that Vyasa Rishi may have been inspired by a royal interfamily battle that took place in the region between the ninth and fourteenth centuries B.C.

Speaking of the Gita in the Mahabharata, Mahatma Gandhi adds, "Even in 1888-89, when I first became acquainted with the Gita, I felt that it was not a historical work, but that under the guise of physical warfare, it described the duel that perpetually went on in the hearts of mankind, and that physical warfare was brought in merely to make the description of the internal duel more alluring. ... Krishna of the Gita is perfection and right knowledge personified. ... Man is not at peace with himself till ... self-realization. This self-realization is the subject of the Gita, as it is of all scriptures."[111]

By setting it against the backdrop of a battle, Vyasa Rishi also captured the senselessness of warfare, and questioned the glorification of martial virtues. Some scholars believe that Vyasa Rishi and the writers who followed him may have been influenced by Buddhism, Jainism, and Emperor Ashoka's sense of revulsion after the battle for the Kingdom of Kalinga.[112]

Mahatma Gandhi says, "The author of the Mahabharata has not established the necessity of physical warfare; on the contrary, he has proved its futility. He has made the victors shed tears of sorrow and repentance, and has left them nothing but a legacy of miseries."[113]

RAMAYANA

The other great epic, the Ramayana, also stresses faithfulness, love, truth, and good over evil. It is a story of one of the *avatars* of Vishnu, Rama, who triumphs over the demonic king Ravana. Leaving his kingdom of Ayodhya, Rama goes into exile for fourteen years. During the exile, Rama encounters Ravana, a demon. Eventually, Rama restores goodness by killing the evil forces represented by Ravana.

Historians believe that the Ramayana was composed after the Mahabharata, even though its story may be of an earlier period, possibly of around 4000 to 1500 B.C. Valmiki, a great *rishi* and a poet, compiled the twenty-four thousand verses of the Ramayana sometime in the period of 400 to 200 B.C.

***

Valmiki Rishi divided the Ramayana into seven *khandas*, "parts." The first part, Bala Khand, captures Rama's childhood and youth. He is the eldest of King Dasharatha's four sons. By breaking Shiva's bow, an impossible feat for a mere mortal, he wins the hand of Sita for marriage.

Part 2, the Ayodhya Khand, sets the stage for Rama's banishment to the wilderness. When the aging King Dasharatha of Ayodhya decides to consecrate Rama as heir apparent, the king's second wife, Kaikeyi, forces her husband to honor a promise he had made long ago. The promise was to grant her any wish she had. She asked to exile Rama for fourteen years and to place her own son, Bharat, on the throne. The part ends with the departure of Rama, his wife, Sita, and his brother, Laxman, to the forest. However, despite his mother's wishes, Bharat does not assume the throne. He places Rama's sandals on the throne and acts as Rama's regent during the exile.

The third part, the Aranya Khand, captures the tension with the demonic forces led by the ten-headed Ravana, lord of *rakhsasas*, "demons." Although depicted as a demon, Ravana was a highly literate Brahmin intellectual who through great *tapa*, "intense form of ascetic practice and meditation," had gained invulnerability and ruled over Lanka, the country known as Sri Lanka today. No one, including the gods, could kill him. To make the drama possible, however, a god incarnate in human form could kill him. The Ramayana portrays Ravana as the epitome of *adharma*, "against *dharma*." Ravana raises the stakes by abducting Sita.

The fourth and fifth parts, the Kiskindha and the Sundara Khandas, deal with locating Sita. This is when the popular Hanuman, a monkey of great might who is capable of leaping the oceans, sets out to locate Sita and make contact. The story becomes entertaining when Ravana sets fire to Hanuman's tail to punish him for trying to destroy Lanka. However, this backfires on Ravana. Hanuman, who is immune to burning by fire, has the ability to extend or retract his tail at will.

Hanuman with his extended burning tail leaps from building to building and sets the entire city on fire. After dousing the tail fire in the ocean, Hanuman retracts his tail and safely returns to Rama with a full account of his expedition.

The sixth part, the Yuddha Khand, deals with the killing of Ravana and Sita's rescue and return to Ayodhya as the king. The last part, the Uttara Khand, deals with Sita giving birth to two sons, and Rama's eventual return to the heavens.

Just as Vyasa Rishi depicted the Pandavas as the embodiment of *dharma*, law and justice, and the Kauravas as the epitome of *adharma*, Valmiki Rishi shows Rama as the personification of *dharma* and Ravana as the epithet of *adharma*.

Poet laureate Tulsidas' sixteenth-century version of the Ramayana in Hindi dialect, called Ramacharitmanas, is more popular than Valmiki Rishi's original Sanskrit version. Ramayana is an enormously popular *bhakti* text. Through various festivals, Hindus honor Rama and Krishna, and perpetuate the stories of the Mahabharata and the Ramayana.

FESTIVALS

Festivals are a way to keep the common folks engaged with the faith and keep the community spiritually alive. As such, all faiths have periodic festivals. Hinduism is no different; it has at least one festival of some kind every month.[114]

The majority of Hindu festivals are colorful and informal. Red is an auspicious color; Hindus generally prefer bright and vibrant colors.

Diwali (shortened version of Dipawali, also spelled Deepavali, Deepawali, and Dipavali) is a major Hindu festival, also known as the Festival of Lights. Rows of lights, traditionally with an oil-soaked wick burning in clay lamps, decorate the homes. It is a celebration of the triumph of good over evil. It commemorates the restoration of divine order and light over demonic disorder and darkness. It is also a celebration of Rama's return to Ayodhya after fourteen years of exile, thus ending the evil forces of Ravana. Being a celebration of the conquest of evil forces, it is also a celebration of Krishna's defeat of the demonic Nakasura.

As with everything else in Hinduism, there is flexibility in the way people celebrate the various festivals. At times, different communities put their own twist on the celebrations. For example, in Nepal, Diwali is known as Tihar, and includes Bhai Tika. It is a day when sisters put *tika*, "an auspicious colorful mark" on the forehead, on their brothers for good health and long life. It has a similar significance as sisters attaching *rakhi*, "sacred thread," on their brothers' wrists during the festival of Rakhi, in other parts of India.

Diwali is also an occasion to honor and worship Lakshmi, the goddess of good fortune. Many Hindu businesses consider it the start of a new fiscal year. Hindus celebrate Diwali with gusto and a fireworks display.

Dashera (or Dussera), also known as Bijaya Dashami, and the festival of Navaratri, are also major festivals for the Hindus. They appear more popular in Nepal and in the northern parts of India. It is a celebration of Durga and her many other forms. In Gujarat, the Hindus celebrate Navaratri with Garba dances.

***

Through the festivals, Hindus also attempt to remind the faithful that the *murtis* and the icons are just the Supreme Soul's images that one can directly relate to but in the end, the ultimate reality is the Supreme Soul.

In many cities and villages, during some festivals, the faithful sculpt the figure of a god or goddess in clay, paint him or her with beautiful colors, and dress him or her appropriately so that he or she looks divine. Hundreds of men carry these divine figures around the town in special carriages, thereby allowing the devotees to worship the god or the goddess. Throngs of devotees pack the streets to pay their respects to the deities. However, at the end of the celebration, which may last several days, the devotees carry the divine sculpture to a pond, river, or the sea, where the sculpture made of unbaked clay and natural colors slowly dissipates in the water.

For example, in Kolkata, India, devotees fashion grand images of the goddess Durga in clay during the festival of Durga Puja. They parade the images of the goddess around the town accompanied by festive music. Crowds of people come to worship her. On the final day, they end the festival by immersing the images in the nearby Hoogly River. In Mumbai, devotees fashion beautiful images of Ganesh during the Ganesh Chaturthi, and worship them with great fanfare as Ganapati Bappa for ten days. It is a grand public event with the streets jammed with celebrants. On the tenth day, the devotees immerse the beautiful clay idols in the ocean.

The sculpture, however beautiful and holy, is only a manmade object. It is just an image to depict an aspect of the Supreme Soul. A *murti* or a sculpture, however real looking, is still an image. For the Hindus, the real is the Supreme Soul.

***

At times, different Hindu communities celebrate the same festivals very differently. While Rakhi, also called Raksha Bandan, is a major festival in many parts of India, it is a relatively minor festival in Nepal. In India, girls and young women tie *rakhi* around the wrists of their brothers or other male relatives and friends for their good health and long life, and in return get a present (typically cash) from their male relatives. In Nepal, normally people get the sacred thread tied around their wrist from priests or close male relatives.

Some festivals are unique to certain communities. The festival of Thaipusam includes a ritual known as Kavadi, when some of the devotees pierce their body with skewers or dangle meat hooks from the skin, is unique to certain communities in South India or to people who migrated from there to other countries such as Malaysia.

Hindus even have a festival just for the women. During the festival of Teej, women pray for their husband's long life. They celebrate the festival with dances and feasts.

Many festivals are associated with farming. Pongol is a South Indian four-day festival that honors the gods for the good harvest. The name comes from married women boiling rice pudding until the pot overflows. Naag Panchami is another festival that has its origins with farming. By worshipping *naag*, "the king of the snakes," farmers hope to be spared from snakebites.

Every community in the world appears to have a festival that coincides with the arrival of spring. Hindus have Holi, a jovial celebration during which people smear colored powders and spray colored water on each other.

RITUALS

As mentioned earlier, based on the Griha Sutra, the Dharma Sutra, and the Dharma Sastras, Hindus have compiled a set of rituals honoring the transitional points in people's lives. They call them Hindu *sanskaras*, "traditions," which cover rituals from pre-birth to death.[115]

For example, the *sanskaras* cover rituals used while naming a child (*namakarana*), feeding a baby solid food for the first time (*annaprasana*), the beginning of learning (*vidya arambha*), and rituals when children are old enough to be formally inducted into the faith called *upanayana* or *bratabandha*.[116] They also prescribe the *vivah*, "marriage rituals," and eventually *anteshthi*, "the funeral rites."

Traditionally, *upanayana* was the ritual to induct a Hindu into the *bramahcharya* phase, starting with learning the Gayatri Mantra, investiture with *janeu*, "sacred thread," and finally leaving home to study at the guru's house.[117] In the *bramahcharya* phase, Hindus spent years at the guru's house primarily studying the Vedas, Vedangas, Upavedas, and the various aspects of the *dharma*. Although no one literally leaves home to go to the guru's house these days, the ritual still requires a simulation.

After completing the studies, Hindus returned home, learned the family trade, married, and started the *grihasthi* phase. With the changing culture, many Hindus compress the rituals and conduct some of the *upanayana* rituals at the time of the marriage itself.

Incidentally, until recent times, Gayatri Mantra was considered a sacred *mantra* known only to those who had undergone the *upanayana* ritual.

Unlike in the West where white signifies purity and often is a preferred color for the bride at weddings, a Hindu bride is dressed mostly in red and other bright colors.

Based on the Jyotish Sastra, using the positions of the *navagrahas,* "nine heavenly bodies," Hindu calendars include the days considered auspicious for a wedding.[118] Many Hindus still consult the astrological charts of the groom and the bride to set the most auspicious day for the wedding.[119]

Hindu weddings are very informal and colorful events. Unlike, for example, the Christian weddings, there are no rehearsals of any kind. A Hindu's *vivah,* "marriage," comprises several days of celebrations and rituals.

The Hindu bride and groom jointly walk around the ceremonial fire in the presence of family, friends, and priests to formalize the marriage. From the Vedic times, ceremonial fire and oblations to the sacred fire in a ceremonial fire pit or *homa* have been at the center of many Hindu rituals. Priests chant the Vedic *mantras* in honor of the deity or deities during the *homa*. Besides the Vedic belief that fire carries the oblation to the gods in the heavens, Hindus believe that fire is the ultimate witness as it was there at the creation of the universe and will be there when the universe finally dissolves. Hence, in addition to the family and friends, from the *dharmic* perspective, Hindus consider the fire also a witness to the wedding.

Hindu wedding vows taken jointly by the couple are about mutual well-being, taking care of the family, and the journey of life together. The vows typically include the following:

- Provide a living for family, avoid harmful things, support each other in righteous activities;
- Build physical, mental, and spiritual powers and lead a healthy lifestyle;

- Earn and increase wealth by righteous and proper means;
- Acquire knowledge, happiness, and harmony by mutual love, respect, understanding, and faith;
- Have children, wish for their long lives;
- Share pleasures together;
- Be true to each other, loyal, and remain lifelong companions by this wedlock.

Although every married Hindu couple has agreed to a version of these vows by giving their consent in front of family, friends, and priests, they may not be fully aware of the vows themselves. Typically, the officiating priest rapidly chants all these vows in Sanskrit, which most of the brides and the grooms do not understand. Often the bride and the groom just repeat whatever the priest tells them to say.

***

When a person dies, the *praan*, "the energy of the soul," leaves the body. After death, the body is cremated so that all the components revert to Prakriti. To avoid any possibility of the soul lingering around its discarded shell, Hindus try to cremate the dead body as soon as practically possible.

The thirteen-day rite of *anteshthi* that immediately follows death is based mostly on Puranic *bhakti* rituals intended to expedite the soul's travel to the heavens. Mourners typically dress in white. As a sign of respect to the departed soul, family rituals also include a mourning period that can last up to a year, followed by yearly *shraddha*, "anniversary death rites."

Mourning relatives and well-wishers often quote the following passage from Gita 2.22 in their message of condolence:

> Just as a man sheds worn-out garments and puts on other new ones, likewise the embodied soul casts off worn-out bodies and enters into others, which are new.

WORSHIP AND PILGRIMAGE

Even though a verse in the Shiva Puran says, "The highest state is the natural realization of God's presence, the second in rank is meditation and contemplation, the third is the worship of symbols which are reminders of the Supreme, and the fourth is performance of ritual and pilgrimages to sacred places," many *bhaktas* put a higher premium on worship, rituals, and pilgrimage.[120]

Not only do the Hindus accept flexibility in the pursuit of the Supreme Soul, but they also accept flexibility in the way they dress, their preferences for foods, and how they worship. For example, while many Hindus may put a red *tika* or *tilak*, "a small dot," on the forehead as a symbol of God's blessing, some Hindus, especially the Shiva *bhaktas* in South India, have *tripundra*, "three ash (*bivuti*) lines," on their forehead. Besides being a symbol of God's blessing, *tripundra* is a reminder of the transitory nature of life and the need to seek *moksha*. Although there are many interpretations of the three ash lines in *tripundra*, turning one's ego, *karma*, and illusion of *maya* to ashes and seeking inner purity is probably the most plausible one. Shiva worshippers coming out of the Pashupatinath Temple in Nepal will have a small paste of sandalwood on their forehead.

Hindus can be vegetarians or non-vegetarians with further subclassifications. Possibly influenced by Ayurveda, on certain days of the year, some refrain from having food with salt, and the non-vegetarians avoid meat.

On special holy days, Hindus may fast. However, fasting means different things to different people. Some may limit themselves to fruits, some to just water, and others may abstain even from a drop of water from sunrise to sunset.

Following Vaishnavism, Shaivism, or Shaktism, a Hindu may worship Vishnu, Shiva, or Shakti. Alternatively, a Hindu may decide to worship all of them. A Smarta worships Vishnu, Shiva, Durga, Ganesh, and Surya, the Sun god.

Although the prime focus of the religious life is the home and most Hindus worship their chosen deity at home, they also visit the temples. At home, it could be the grand *murtis* of the deities in a special room with marble floors or just a five-cent poster of the god's image dangling from a rusty nail on the kitchen wall of a mud hut.

Hindus often recite the *slokas*, "the hymns that rhyme," from the *stotras* (also spelled *stotrams*). *Stotras* are mostly prayers or devotional literatures related to a deity. Some *stotras* include the many names for a deity, which some Hindus chant as a part of their daily prayers.

Worshipping the deity in a temple often includes *parikrama* or *pradakshana*, "going around the deity's *murti*," often saying some kind of a prayer or singing hymns while walking around the *murti*, and ringing bells (*ghanta*). After walking around the deity, the devotees normally stand in front of the *murti* and pray. Typically, the worship includes *anjali*, "paying homage to the god with folded hands"; most often, the devotees hold flowers inside their folded hands.

The worship can also include *arati*, "honoring the deity with light." At the end of the worship, the priest may put a *tika* on the devotee, and give the devotee some flowers and *prasad* that have come in close contact with the *murti* of the deity. Typically, the *prasad* includes some kind of sweets or fruit.

Incidentally, Hindus use the right hand (with the left hand normally touching it) when putting a *tika* on others. They normally use both hands while making an offering to the deities. During the *parikrama,* the devotees walk around the deity's *murti* in a clockwise direction, placing the deity always on the right of the devotee. Although some see a connection with the rightward movements of the celestial bodies and the importance of the right hand in palmistry, the practice may be just a custom that right-handed people started thousands of years ago. After all, right-handed people constitute the overwhelming majority in most societies.

Hindus have no special time or day of the week to visit the temple. They can visit the temple and worship the deity any time of the day and as often as they wish. It is up to each devotee to decide how he or she wants to pursue the path to his or her own *moksha*.

To keep the faith front and center in people's lives, and help the faithful spiritually connect with the deity for whom the temple is dedicated, some temples or groups closely associated with the temples, mostly in eastern and southern India, have classical temple dances. These dances are rich with devotional expression, and extol the virtues of the deity.

Depending on the region, the temples can look very different. Invariably, whereas the *murti* of the god or goddess will be in the inner sanctum, the look of the outer structures can vary greatly. For example, the temples in Nepal and the Himalayan region have uniquely Nepalese pagoda-style architecture; the temples in southern India often have the *gopura* or *gopurams*, "gateways."

Gopuras are elaborately carved structures with details related to the powers and feats of the deity to whom the temple is dedicated. Temples built by the South Indian communities outside India also have *gopuras*.

Sensual and erotic sculptures often adorn the outer structures of many temples. Hindus visit temples to pay homage to the god whose *murti* is placed in the inner sanctum.

Even the inner sanctum can look different. While some temples may have beautiful and ornate *murtis*, others may have just a rounded stone; it is all about what one perceives to be sacred.

In many villages, the devotees worship with equal devotion a smooth stone on the trunk of a tree. Normally the tree is a *pipal* (also spelled *peepul, peepal*), a variety of tree normally found in the region.[121] Hindus regard the *pipal* as a symbol of longevity and regeneration.

***

Hindus consider the rivers sacred. The seven most sacred are the Ganga (Ganges), Yamuna, Saraswati, Narmada, Godavari, Kaveri, and Sindhu (Indus). Even though the river Saraswati dried up centuries ago, devotees believe that the river is still there but has gone underground.

Hindus regard the Ganga as the holiest of them all. As per the Puranic legends, Bhagirathi Rishi brought the river from the heavens to Earth. The river emerges near the glacier in Gangotri in the Himalayas and ends in the Bay of Bengal. Hindus call it *Ganga Maata*, "Mother Ganga," possibly because of their reliance on the river for farming in the fertile Gangetic plains. The river has major pilgrimage centers on its banks or nearby.

Every so many years, Hindus have major gathering of pilgrims at some of the holy locations on the banks of the Ganga River, or at the confluence of rivers. For example, nearly every three years millions of pilgrims travel great distances to bathe in the holy river during the festival of Kumbha Mela.

There are many legends behind the Kumbha Mela. According to one of them, Kumbha was the pot holding the nectar of immortality from the Puranic churning of the mythical ocean. When the gods tried to grab the pot, four drops of nectar fell to Earth over the cities of Hardwar, Prayag (a city in north India called Allahabad today), Ujjain, and Nasik. The Kumbha Melas alternate between these four locations, and start the new cycle every twelve years.

The Kumbha Mela in the sixth year is called Ardha Kumbha Mela, and the one in the twelfth year is called Purna Kumbha Mela, which always takes place in Prayag. The twelfth Purna Kumbha Mela is known as the Maha Kumbha Mela, which obviously comes only every 144 years. *Ardha* means "half," *purna* means "full," and *maha* means "great."

The last Maha Kumbha Mela was in 2001 in Prayag at the *tribeni sangam*, "confluence of the three rivers": the Ganga, Yamuna, and Saraswati. Reportedly, more than seventy million Hindus participated in the forty-four days of Maha Kumbha Mela. The Purna Kumbha Mela of 2013 that started on January 14 and lasted for fifty-five days is estimated to have attracted somewhere between eighty million to one hundred million pilgrims at the *tribeni sangam*, making it one of the largest gatherings in world history.[122]

***

Many Hindus go on pilgrimage. *Tirthayatra* is very popular with the Hindus.

Tirtha means "a ford" or "a crossing"—the crossing to the heavens from a connecting point on Earth. The connecting point is the *dham*, "the sacred site." Hence, *Tirthayatra* means "pilgrimage to a sacred place, which connects to the heavens."

Char Dham, the four holy places in the four corners of India—Badrinath in the north, Rameshwaram in the south, Puri in the east, and Dwarika in the west—are major places for Hindu pilgrimage.[123] Hindus worship Vishnu as Naranarayana in Badrinath, Rama in Rameshwaram, Krishna as Jaggannath in Puri, and Krishna at his old capital, Dwarika.

In addition to these, there are regional groups of holy places such as the Char Dham in the Himalayan group, Mahabharata's seven *dhams,* up to 108 sacred Shakti Pithas, the Shaiva Jyotirlinga networks, Vaishnava sites, and the regional networks such as the Murukan-Palani.[124]

***

Just like everything else in Hinduism, one can visit all these pilgrimage sites many times over or never set foot in one. One can conform to all the outwardly signs and symbols of religiosity, follow all the rituals, or comply with none. One can study all or none of the *sutras* and the *sastras.* One can believe in all the gods or not believe in any of them. One can perceive the gods as the aspects of Brahman or Brahman itself. It is all about the freedom to choose. One is the master of one's destiny and *karma* as Gita 18.63 says, "Do as you choose," after reflecting fully.[125] After learning everything about the *dharma,* one has to find one's own path to *moksha.*

7

PATHS TO *MOKSHA*

According as one acts, so does one become. One becomes virtuous by virtuous action, bad by bad action.

—Upanishad

$\mathcal{H}$induism believes in the Supreme, who is omnipotent and is in charge of everything. However, omnipotence does not mean irrationality.[126] The laws dictate the creation of the universe and the functioning of everything within it. The laws of *karma* dictate how one frees the soul and attains *moksha*.

Hindus believe in *karma*, "the consequence of every action and every thought." It is the law of cause and effect. Each individual creates his or her own spiritual destiny by his or her thoughts, words, and deeds. Not only do the Hindus agree with the saying "Whatsoever a man soweth, that shall he also reap," but they also go one step further and say, "Whatsoever a man reaps, that he must have sown."[127]

Karma is an outcome of the past merit and demerit. The Mahabharata says that the inner self is the judge; there is no external judge to reward or punish us.[128]

Karma survives *sansaar*, "the world of a continuous cycle of life followed by death." Most Hindus believe that one's present fate is a result of one's past. However, one can change it; one is the architect of one's own fate and the builder of one's own destiny. Gita 4.37 says, "As fire burns all fuel to ashes, the fire of wisdom turns all *karma* to ashes."

While every good *karma* erases the bad one and gets one closer to attaining inner peace, the *klesas*, "impairments of the mind and affliction," perpetuate the *karmic* bondage. Patanjali Rishi's Yoga Sutra 2.3 lists the following five *klesas*:

- *Avidya*   Ignorance of the real, the Supreme Soul
- *Ashmita*   Ego
- *Raga*   Attachments
- *Dwesa*   Aversion
- *Abhinivesa*   Clinging to life as if it never ends, fear of extinction

Avidya is the cause of the other four *klesas*.

In Hinduism, humanity's problem is *avidya*, and self-identification with the ego; for example, in Christianity, it is moral rebellion. Christians seek forgiveness of sin and reconciliation with Jesus, whereas the Hindus seek to get rid of their ego and gain the wisdom to realize their inner divinity.

Incidentally, because of their ability to think in a rational way, Hindus believe that, among all the living creatures on Earth, only humans can free themselves from the *karmic* bondage and find their way to *moksha*.

***

Hinduism has advocated for thousands of years that the sense organs—eyes, nose, ears, taste buds, skin—are only the external receptors of the *indriyas*. Eyes are just organs, but eyes do not see; dead people still have eyes but cannot see. The real seats of perception are the *indriyas*.

Moreover, Hinduism says that when one sees or smells the fragrance of a flower, it is the flower's *tanmatras*, "the fine particles," that react with the *indriyas*. *Tanmatras* are known today as vibrating atoms with their electromagnetic fields. *Indriyas* would be the centers of sense perceptions such as the visual cortex, auditory cortex, and postcentral gyrus, which is the primary sensory cortex associated with sensations from the skin.

Hinduism talks about *sukshma sharira*, "subtle or finer body," and *bhutas*, "gross matter."[129] The gross matter builds the *sthula sharira*, "physical body." The finer body is where the conscious and subconscious mind, *gunas* and *indriyas*, meet.

Hinduism says that neither the finer body nor the physical body is active by itself. Just as Shakti is the energy of Brahman that activates the universe, *praan* (also spelled *prana*) is the energy of the individual soul that activates the physical and the finer body. Instead of saying, "He or she is dead," the common Hindu expression is "His or her *praan* left."

Hindus believe that each work one does and each thought one thinks produces *samskara*, "an impression on the mind."[130] The sum total of these impressions shapes one's spiritual destiny.

Karmic balance leads to total inner peace. When the soul leaves, the physical body dies. If *karma* is not resolved, then the soul encased by the *karma saaya*, "*karmic* residues," re-enters the body of a newborn. The *karma saaya* contains the *vasana*, "fragrance," of the finer body when it leaves. Gita 15.8 says:

> Just as the wind carries the perfumes from their source,
> so too the soul takes the fragrances when it leaves, and
> migrates them to the new body.

***

The fragrance of the finer body from the previous life affects the temperament of the newborn.

Vasistha's Yoga, which was written probably more than two thousand years ago, says, "The tendencies brought forward from past incarnations [*vasanas* captured by the *karmic* residues] are of two kinds—pure and impure. The pure ones lead you towards liberation, and the impure ones invite trouble. ... You are not impelled to action by anything other than yourself. Hence, you are free to strengthen the pure latent tendencies in preference to the impure ones. The impure ones have to be abandoned gradually and the mind turned away from them little by little, lest there should be violent reaction. By encouraging the good tendencies to act repeatedly strengthen them. The impure ones will weaken by disuse."[131]

Many Hindus blame fate for their situation in the present life. However, Vasistha's Yoga refutes it:

One who says 'Fate is directing me to do this' is brainless.
…
People use such expressions as 'I am impelled by fate or divine dispensation to do this' for self-satisfaction, but this not true. For example, if an astrologer predicts that a young man would become a great scholar, does that young man become a scholar without study? No. … All of us have attained self-knowledge by self-effort alone. … Fate is nothing but the culmination of one's own action.[132]

Based on some of Hinduism's holy books, many Hindus believe that one is born into a prosperous family or has good health because of good *karma* in the previous lives. Although such beliefs provide an explanation to the inequality of birth and encourage people to follow the *dharma*, this notion appears illogical.

It is very unlikely that *karma* has anything to do with wealth, material status, or even health. By definition, *karma* should reflect the level of inner peace, how close one is in realizing one's divinity within. Accordingly, some are born with more inner peace or a peaceful temperament than others are.

Parents provide the seed to create the physical body, which besides the external features also includes the mind and intelligence. The difference between identical twins at birth is the contribution from the essence of the finer body from the previous life or the temperament.

The temperament colors one's life. While the environment can influence the mind, one's temperament affects how one reacts to ego, revenge, envy, anger, sloth, gluttony, lust, greed, and pride.

As genes adapt to the demands of the temperament, certain genes may be switched on and others switched off. Consequently, identical twins born with exactly the same DNA may differ genetically by the time they get to old age.

However, one does not have to be a prisoner of the *karma saaya* from the past lives. As Vasistha's Yoga says, one can change these tendencies brought forward from past incarnations. One is truly the architect of one's life.

***

The temperament or the tendencies brought forward from past incarnations are the same as the *gunas* described by the Sankhya *darshana*. As discussed earlier, whether it is the universe itself or an individual, everything in Prakriti is subject to the varying combinations of the three *gunas*. While *rajas* and *tamas* represent the repulsive force and the force of contraction at the universal scale, at the individual level *rajas* represents activities tainted by selfish desires, the quest for power, and restlessness, and *tamas* represents base animal instincts, dullness, and violence.

Wealth, power, pride, and glory give a person with *rajas gunas* happiness, whereas people with *tamas gunas* find happiness in violence, lethargy, subduing others, and enjoying other people's suffering. *Sattwa* represents goodness, joy, calmness, and selflessness. The Gita says:

> *Sattwa*, *rajas* and *tamas*—the three *gunas* of Prakriti tie down the imperishable soul to the body. (Gita 14.5)

> Wisdom follows from *sattwa*. Being pure, it is illuminating, untainted, and conditioned by a sense of happiness and knowledge. ... A *sattwika* is free from attachment, unegotistic, full of resolution and vigor, unmoved by success or failure. (Gita 14.6, 18.26)

> Being born of unlimited desires and longings, and swayed by passion ... a *rajasika* seeks the fruit of actions, and is greedy. Being oppressive by nature and of impure conduct is affected by joy and sorrow. (Gita 14.7, 18.27)

> Born of stupor and ignorance ... lacking piety, self-control, a *tamashika* is uncultured, arrogant, deceitful, malicious, slothful, downhearted, procrastinating, and inclined to rob others of their livelihood. (Gita 14.8, 18.28)

Hindus have been aware of the mind-body connection for nearly three thousand years. Maitreya Upanishad 1.9 says that a person becomes what he or she thinks. Hindus, in normal conversation, often quote the Sanskrit *sloka*, which says, "You are what you think."[133]

Hence, if one does not like to be angry with someone, all the person has to do is change the thought from anger to maybe a thought of compassion. Patanjali Rishi's Yoga Sutra 2.33 says, "To be free from the thoughts that distract you from Yoga, you must cultivate thoughts of opposite kind."

The goal in life is to train the mind to subdue the *rajas* and *tamas*, and move toward *sattwa* by nurturing inner qualities such as patience and forbearance, contentment, self-discipline, generosity, and compassion. Hindus believe that when the *rajas* and *tamas* are subdued, people with *rajas* become more affectionate, compassionate, and loving, while people with *tamas* develop a more temperate nature. Upon attaining *sattwa*, *karmic* residues disappear, and the soul becomes free.

Hindus appear enamored with the word *sattwa*. They even have a *sattwic* diet, which includes items such as whole grains, legumes, fresh fruit, green and colorful vegetables.

Gurus often advocate cultivating positive thinking, maintaining a pleasant demeanor, refraining from blaming others, and sacrificing pride. One highly respected *swami* in Nepal even wants his followers to laugh, and laugh a lot.[134]

Physiologically, the body releases "feel-good" chemicals such as endorphins during laughter. Such chemicals can help lower one's blood pressure and decrease one's heart rate.

One has one's entire lifetime to subdue the undesirable *gunas*, move toward *sattwa*, and attain *moksha* or *mukti*. One who attains *mukti* while still alive is called a *jivanmukta*.[135]

As discussed earlier, Hinduism divides a person's life into four phases: unmarried, householder, retirement, and renunciation. Although some follow *nivritti marga*, "path of renunciation," most of the Hindus abide by these four phases, following the path of *pravritti marga*, "path of worldly life."

People who follow the *pravritti marga* do not try to fight against nature, but, wherever feasible, attempt to satisfy its basic demands, which will help quiet the mind and help subdue *rajas* and *tamas*. They believe that denying something only adds to the craving.

Followers of *pravritti marga* work toward developing their full potential, making money, having a family, and enjoying all the materialistic pleasures. Hindus often quote the Sanskrit version of the following saying:

> Wealth and knowledge should be acquired by every moment and by every grain.
> How can knowledge be gained if moment is lost? How can wealth be accumulated if a grain is wasted?[136]

However, Hinduism encourages moderation and cautions the followers of *pravritti marga* against obsession, too much attachment, and unbridled cravings. Almost every Hindu holy book speaks of the insatiable nature of cravings and desires; cravings lead to unending pursuit of fleeting pleasures, and unfulfilled desires result in unhappiness. Swami Adiswarananda says:

> "The secret of a happy life is freedom from dependence. As long as we need something or someone to make us happy, we are at the mercy of that thing or person and, therefore, miserable."[137]

Interestingly, Albert Einstein echoes a similar sentiment, "If you want to live a happy life, tie it to a goal, not to people or objects."[138]

Hinduism encourages people to follow *dharma* at every moment of life. It says death can snatch them away anytime, "Follow *dharma* and abide by good conduct, as if the death is holding you by the tufts of your hair."[139]

***

Hinduism does not condemn the rich or extol poverty as a virtue in itself. It allows one to accumulate wealth in a rightful way. However, obsessed with all the trappings of wealth, social status, and conspicuous consumption to the extreme, many often forget the "rightful way" part and pursue wealth by any means.

Hinduism tries to seek a balance and encourages the faithful to live a full life with the four phases or the *pravritti marga*, but it does not stop them from choosing their own paths if they so wish. Hindus, who skip the *pravritti marga*, renouncing the attractions of materialism, follow the *nivritti marga* and lead a celibate life. *Sadhus* or *sanyasis*, "ascetics," which includes the naked holy men smeared in ashes, follow the *nivritti marga*.

Although most Hindus associate *sanyas* with ascetics who focus on the outer symbols of robes, walking staff, bodies smeared in ashes, and wandering around the holy sites blowing a conch shell, the essence of *sanyas* lies in treating everyone alike, being peaceful in the midst of chaos, and remaining pure amid impurities. Instead of the visible outer symbols, *sanyas* or asceticism is about inner transformation, renunciation of the outer trappings of life, and leading a life of deep spiritual contemplation.

The ascetics with their bodies smeared in ashes are a novelty in the West. Their Yoga poses adorn Western magazines.

***

Whenever people refer to Yoga in the Western world, they are mostly referring to various *asanas* and *pranayama*. The *asanas* often incorporate postures to slowly and methodically strengthen the body and improve overall balance.

For the Hindus, meditation is an integral part of Yoga. For thousands of years, Hindus have used Yoga's meditation techniques to seek inner peace. Meditation can relax and settle the mind, and replace negative thoughts and emotions with positive ones.

Yoga means "a yoke" or "a link." To the Hindus, Yoga is a connecting link between the spiritual aspirant and the Supreme Soul, and there can be an infinite number of connecting links. Hinduism does not believe in the "one-size-fits-all" concept.

As mentioned at the beginning of this book, like a bird flying from point A to point B, Hinduism focuses on getting to point B—connecting with the Supreme Soul and attaining *moksha*—rather than the path taken to get to point B. Depending on the cerebral, emotional, and devotional makeup, it is up to each person to find the right path for his or her own *moksha* or *mukti*. Hinduism lists four distinct paths or *margas* while recognizing the possibility of other paths that may be an even better fit for some.

PATH OF DEVOTION (BHAKTI YOGA OR BHAKTI MARGA)

The faithful who follow the Path of Devotion see the god or goddess with physical characteristics and qualities they can relate to in their daily lives. This is ideal for people who prefer to develop a frame of mind that generates a feeling of closeness to their god or goddess, who is full of love and compassion, and who will protect and take care of them. They perceive a god or goddess who will reward them for doing the right things and admonish them for not listening or doing things that are not permitted. They seek grace from the god or goddess of their devotion, which could be Shiva, Krishna, Rama, or Mahadevi.

Speaking of Krishna, Gita 18.62 says:

> Take shelter in Him alone with all your being. By His grace, you shall attain supreme peace and the eternal abode.

However, the *bhaktas* should be worthy of the grace.

Bhaktas seek God's grace by concentrating the mind on the loving God. They develop an intense spiritual love for God while maintaining physical and mental purity. Some Hindus believe that the god or goddess will reciprocate his or her grace on the *bhaktas* who show their grace to their fellow living beings.

As their spiritual love for God increases, other worldly attachments gradually decline. One starts to detach from the materialistic attachments, greed, and ego as the inner serenity starts to take hold.

Bhaktas are encouraged to chant holy names (*japa*), sing devotional songs, constantly remember God, show adoration, and worship. They mostly listen to devotional music, which tends to foster inner calmness.

Some may find pursuits such as playing musical instruments, taking care of birds and animals, and gardening equally peaceful.

As one advances in *bhakti*, one's worship changes from external and ritualistic to mental. *Bhaktas* spend more time meditating on God without uttering the words aloud.

The Gita gives details of how the Bhakti Yogi should meditate to the god of their devotion:

> Having firmly placed the seat in a spot, which is free from dirt and other impurities, concentrating the mind and controlling the functions of the mind and senses, one should practice Yoga for self-purification. Holding the body, head and neck in a straight line, erect and motionless, one should fix the gaze on the tip of the nose, without looking in other directions. … Tranquil and with the mind disciplined and fixed on Me [Krishna], one should sit absorbed in Me. Thus constantly applying his mind to Me, the one of disciplined mind attains the everlasting peace, consisting of supreme bliss, which abides in Me. (Gita 6.11–15)

However, those who subscribe to the Vedic Bhakti believe that priestly rituals and offerings to the gods will lead them to *moksha*.

Upon the attainment of *moksha*, at which point the believers of the formless and without attributes Brahman see their souls merging with Brahman, followers of the Bhakti Marga see themselves in the heavens in the presence of their loving God. They do not see themselves merging into their God of devotion. They believe that just because one loves sugar does not mean that one wants to be sugar.

***

While generally considered a branch of Bhakti Yoga, Shakti *bhaktas*, commonly known as Tantrics, who perceive the human body as the microcosm of the spiritual universe and visualize the process of increased spiritual awareness taking place within the body itself, follow a path that includes elements of Raja Yoga.

They believe that Shakti, which is the infinite creative energy of the Supreme that activates the universe, resides in every human being as *kundalini.* Most Tantrics see Shiva as the Supreme, and Shakti as the feminine aspect of Shiva.

Tantrics visualize *kundalini* as a coiled serpent lying dormant at the base *chakra.* They believe that there are seven *chakras.* The lowest *chakra* is located at the end of the spinal cord, and the seventh one is on top of the head. Tantrics envision *chakras* as the center of spiritual energy within a person's body, and believe in progressively awakening them. *Chakras* are essentially Tantrics' steps to *moksha.*

Tantrics believe that the Sushumna channel connects the seven *chakras.* On the left and right of this channel are two other channels, Ida and Pingala. They believe that the normal energy in the body flows through the Ida and Pingala channels. The Sushumna channel, which is blocked, is independent and not connected to the other channels. The rise of *kundalini* clears the blockage in the Sushumna channel.

Tantrics believe in waking up *kundalini,* making it rise up through the various *chakras* to experience an increased spiritual awareness. As the *kundalini* rises up the Sushumna channel and opens the seventh *chakra,* the Tantric will free the soul and attain *moksha.*

The Yogic manipulation of *kundalini* probably started around the eighth century A.D. Today, many refer to this Tantric *sadhana,* "spiritual practice," as Kundalini Yoga or Tantric Yoga.

The *sadhana* is normally accessible through *diksha,* "an initiation ritual using *mantras* under the direction of a guru." *Tantras* are Tantrics' holy books.[140] Tantrics generally believe that by pronouncing the *mantra* in the correct manner, they will gain special power that will lead them to the highest bliss.

The *sadhana* also insists on holiness and purity of all things. It requires its followers to refrain from various forbidden objects such as wine, meat, fish, and sexual intercourse.

While all the spiritual paths discourage temptations, Tantric *sadhana* requires the followers to directly face the forbidden objects and practice their ability to subdue their urges. Some of the sexual practices, food habits, or other steps adopted by the Tantrics to subdue the mind and the basic desires of the flesh can be bewildering.

Some Indologists believe that the erotic carvings outside the many Hindu temples may have their roots in the Tantric influence in Hinduism.

As the *kundalini* rises up, it opens up the following *chakras*, leading to inner peace and *moksha*:

1.	Muladhara (base *chakra*):	It deals with the basic survival needs such as food and shelter. When one is no longer pursuing the desire to own a better home, taste better food, and wear better clothes, or is no longer worried about losing these basic needs, and attains a balance, this *chakra* opens and lets the energy flow through.
2.	Swadhisthana (sacral *chakra*):	It is about procreation. Only when one is in balance and no longer desires a more romantic love or a sexier mate, this *chakra* opens up.
3.	Manipura (solar plexus *chakra*):	It is about one's relationship with others. When one is no longer pursuing the desire to dominate others, this *chakra* opens up.
4.	Anahata (heart *chakra*):	It opens up when one is compassionate.
5.	Vishuddha (throat *chakra*):	It opens up when one is more inclined to listen than talk, and is prone to introspection and self-analysis, truthful in speech, pleasant, and tranquil.

6. Ajna (eyebrow   It opens up when one is be-
   chakra or third eye):   yond ego and emotions, feels
                          beyond the body, realizes the
                          divine love, and gains spiri-
                          tual wisdom. (Also spelled
                          Agya)

7. Sahasrara   When it opens up, one attains
   (crown *chakra*):   *samadhi* or the final realiza-
                          tion of the ultimate and at-
                          tainment of *moksha.*

Some even relate the seven *chakras* to the seven colors of the rainbow with red for the Muladhara, and violet at the other end of the spectrum with the Sahasrara. Some see a connection between some of the *chakras* and the locations of the major endocrine systems.

PATH OF KNOWLEDGE (GYANA YOGA OR GYANA MARGA)

This path is ideal for cerebral types who feel a need to investigate and explore the ultimate truth through their own efforts. The famous quote from the Yajur Veda, "Life is perennial search of truth," is their motto. It allows one to search for the ultimate truth in one's lifetime. One starts with developing an attitude of contentment (*shantosha*) and tranquility of mind (*shanti*), keeping company of the wise (*satsanga*) and then immerses oneself in the rational investigation of the truth (*vichara*).

In the rational investigation of the truth, the person can start at any point, including a blank slate when one does not believe in any god or goddess, or for that matter, even in the existence of the Supreme Soul. Among all the major faiths currently practiced around the world, Hinduism and Buddhism may possibly be the only faiths that include the flexibility not to believe in any god or a supreme being of any kind and let the followers seek the truth for themselves.

The process normally starts with asking the ultimate questions, which the Hindus believe are important for the person's spiritual development. The questions range from "Why do I exist?", "What am I here for?", and "Who am I?" to "What happens when I die?"

The process involves three steps: *shravana*, "hearing"; *manana*, "critical thinking"; and *nididhyasana*, "meditating on the Self." *Shravana* starts with setting the foundation by hearing or learning from the teacher. *Manana* requires one to question and reflect on everything one has heard or learned (even from the teacher) and come to one's own conclusion.

The objective is to nullify everything that is not real or the ultimate truth. The exact words in Sanskrit are "*neti, neti,*" which means "not this, not that." It is a process of logically eliminating things that are not real. Incidentally, the Brihadaranyaka Upanishad frequently uses the concept of *neti, neti,* and peels the layers one at a time.

Manana forces one to go deeper into issues. Hindus believe that through the process of rational inquiry of *manana*, one will eventually recognize one's true self, which leads to the realization of *tat twam asi*.

In the third step, *nididhyasana,* one meditates on *tat*, "That." Years of *nididhyasana* will fuse "I" into "That." The Gyana Yogi will connect with the Supreme and attain *moksha*.

PATH OF ACTION (KARMA YOGA OR KARMA MARGA)

Gita 5.12 says that the devoted soul, having abandoned the result of action, attains complete peace. Karma Yoga is the path of selfless action. It is about fulfilling one's duty as necessity dictates without seeking personal gratification.

Hindus use Arjuna's example from the Gita to illustrate this path. Even though Arjuna objected to fighting his close relations, his duty required him to fight the evil, right the wrong, and follow the path of the right action or Karma Yoga.

This path is ideal for people who do unselfish work without any expectation of reward. The person acts without attachment and accepts the outcome with equanimity. While the Karma Yogis have to be active and action oriented, they have to maintain non-attachment at the same time, which often can be difficult. To address this, Karma Yoga recommends that the aspirant meditate on duty and retain calmness of mind.

Hindus believe that when all the energy is fully devoted to selfless work, people lose all sense of attachment to materialism, greed, and ego. The selfless work itself turns into work for spiritual advancement. It leads to inner peace, realization of the soul, and *moksha.*

Mahatma Gandhi was a Karma Yogi, who devoted his life to India's freedom from British rule without seeking any personal reward. If Mother Teresa had been a Hindu rather than a devout Catholic, she also would be a good example of someone following this path.

PATH OF MEDITATION (DHYANA YOGA OR DHYANA MARGA, ALSO CALLED RAJA YOGA)

As mentioned earlier, Patanjali Rishi developed this Yoga, commonly known today as the Raja Yoga. According to Gita 6.34–35, "The mind is very unsteady, fickle, tenacious, obstinate and powerful ... the mind is restless no doubt, and difficult to curb, but it can be controlled by constant practice of meditation and by the exercise of non-attachment."

Raja Yoga stops the vagaries of the mind. Patanjali Rishi advocated that only a disciplined and structured method of concentration could bring inner peace.

Patanjali Rishi says that when the mind finally settles, it will reveal the true nature of the Supreme Soul. Gita 5.27–28 say:

> Shutting out all external sense objects, with the gaze fixed
> between the eyebrows, having regulated the outgoing

and the ingoing breaths flowing within the nostrils, one who has brought the senses, mind and intellect under control—such a contemplative soul intent on liberation and free from desire, fear and anger, is ever liberated.

Following is the Raja Yoga's eight-step program leading to *moksha*:

1. *Yama*: It is about inner restraint and *ahimsa*, "non-violence in words, deeds, and thoughts," or non-injury to other living creatures mentally and physically.

2. *Niyama*: Requires one to develop self-discipline, internal control, and calmness, and to lead a moral life with truthfulness and purity in thought.

3. *Asana*: It deals with the particular postures of the body, hands, and feet. The seating postures should be firm and comfortable with the spinal column erect and lined up with the neck and head, and with the chest extended out. The seating posture should allow one to sit motionless for an hour or more.

4. *Pranayama*: Breathing is associated with the activity of the mind; the rhythm of breathing can change the rhythm of the brain. It involves various techniques of breathing air in, holding it for a certain time, and the techniques of breathing it out.

5. *Pratyahara*: It is the conscious attempt to withdraw the mind from the physical world that stimulates it, to control the senses, and to

shut out the outside world. Gita 2.58 says, "One, who withdraws the senses from the sense-objects as a tortoise draws in its limbs from all directions, has a stable mind." Techniques include breath control to withdraw from all the senses, and exercises to control restlessness of the mind and manage the bubbling up of extraneous thoughts. With practice, the bubbling of thoughts slows down and the mind starts to settle down and will be prepared to tackle the next three steps.

6. *Dharana*: With intense concentration on an object, the mind becomes calmer and steadier. It will be able to focus better on an object of concentration. This step will automatically flow into the next step, *dhyana*.

7. *Dhyana*: *Dhyana* means "meditation." By this stage, the mind is fully stabilized and able to meditate on an object of choice without any interruption.

8. *Samadhi*: Years of *dhyana* lead to a state of mind when the self and the object of meditation slowly melt away. The mind automatically starts tapping at its core—the soul. This is the stage when one connects with the soul and hence, the Supreme Soul, leading to utmost peace and inner calm—a state of bliss or *ananda* and *moksha*.

***

As mentioned earlier, Hinduism does not compel anyone to follow any path. One can follow any of the four paths above, any combinations of the four paths, or a newer path one has found to be even better.

More than a century ago, Swami Vivekananda said, "Each soul is potentially divine. The goal is to manifest this divinity within by controlling nature, external and internal. Do this either by work [Karma Yoga] or worship [Bhakti Yoga] or psychic control [Raja Yoga] or philosophy [Gyana Yoga]—by one or more or all of these—and be free [free the soul]. This is the whole of religion. Doctrines or dogmas or rituals or books or temples or forms are but secondary details."[141]

8

HINDUS AND HINDUISM TODAY

The best religion is the most tolerant.

—Mme de Giradin

Nearly a billion Hindus inhabit this planet. While there are nearly a couple of million in the United States, more than half a million in the United Kingdom, and a few million spread around the world, mostly in places that were old British colonies, an overwhelming majority of Hindus live on the Indian subcontinent.

Hindus believe that everyone has the divine essence or the God within; one just needs the spiritual eye to see it.

Hindus continue to perceive the formless and without attributes Brahman as the God with form and attributes such as Rama, Krishna, and Shiva, and identify Shakti with Brahman's energy. Besides Brahman, Hindus address the Supreme by various names such as Paramatma, Brahmatma, Parameshwara, Paramshiva, Parabrahma, Purusottama, or just *Om tat sat,* "*Om* that is the truth." *Bhaktas* may add their God's name to this and call him Hari *Om tat sat* or *Om tat* Vishnoi (Vishnu). Hari is one of the names of Krishna.

Most Hindus learn about their *dharma* from the rituals they witness, the worship and the festivals they participate in, the narration of the Puranic stories from their parents, and the coverage of the faith in the media. The priests also generally do not know anything more about the faith beyond the round of rituals they mechanically conduct. As mentioned in the Acknowledgement section of this book, while growing up,

I also just followed the rituals and did not know deeply about my own ancestral faith.

Even though Hindus are aware of the existence of the holy books such as the Vedas, the Upanishads, and the Gita, not many ever read them. Nevertheless, most of them have heard of *tat twam asi* and *ekam sat viprah bahudha vadanti*. They are mindful of the influence of *karma* in this life and future lives, and know the importance of *moksha*.

Hindus mainly follow the ritualistic-priest-centric Vedic practices such as the incantations and rituals of Purva Mimamsa. Normally, it is much easier to follow the rituals, make offerings, and do whatever the priest says than make internal changes to attain inner peace.

Although by definition rituals are acts that do not require a lot of mental engagement, rituals do help perpetuate the *dharmic* tradition and bring families and communities together. As such, every religion includes rituals.

Hindus often donate to temples and reward the priests. While the holy books including the Gita mention *daana*, "donation or charitable giving," possibly because of Hinduism's focus on individuals, the idea of helping the poor and the impoverished in the community is not widely prevalent among Hindus.[142]

Not all Hindus are able to wean themselves eventually out of the attachments to materialism. For some, creating wealth that will last generations takes a higher precedence.

Most Hindus worship the gods and goddesses and chant their holy names (*japa*), follow rituals, sing devotional songs, and go on pilgrimages. In addition to praying for happiness, prosperity, and good health, they believe that the rituals and their devotion to the Almighty will lead them to *moksha*. Some Hindus worship *swamis* and saints as god incarnates.

However, typically in the later phases of their lives, many Hindus appear to recognize the Upanishadic importance of sacrificing ignorance, anger, greed, malice, and ego, and focus more on inner purity than on outer conformity. They complement the external and ritualistic practices of the Vedic Bhakti with the mental disciplines of the Bhakti and Raja Yoga to quiet the mind and attain inner peace.

Even today, Hindus have no concept of heresy or apostasy. Most of them perceive their faith as a spirit of tolerance and willingness to understand and appreciate other points of view based on the realization that the truth is many-sided.[143]

Most Hindus do not believe in "an eye for an eye." They generally subscribe to the notion that one should not commit a *paap* in retaliation for another *paap*.[144] *Paap* is a Sanskrit word that means a sin, a wicked or an evil act.

Hindus come in all varieties—they may be vegetarian or non-vegetarian, pray ten times a day or never pray, follow some beliefs or rituals and not others, worship some gods and not others, or worship all of them. Although centuries ago, Hindu women living near communities with a Muslim majority started to veil themselves, and one still sees Hindu women fully covering their head in some villages in India, Hinduism has no concept of veiling their women nor a requirement for men to keep long beards. Hinduism does not require male or female circumcision. Because it is not a communal religion, there are no group-oriented Friday prayers or Sunday services and no weekly sermons from the pulpit.

The host of the CNN's (USA) television program Global Public Square (GPS), Fareed Zakaria, believes that the Hindus, who constitute more than 80 percent of the Indian population, may have even influenced the thinking of nearly 160 million Indian Muslims. He says, "Islam in India has been altered through its contact with Hinduism, becoming less Abrahamic and more spiritual. Indian Muslims worship saints and shrines, celebrate music and art, and have a more practical outlook on life than many of their coreligionists abroad."[145]

***

Despite having twenty-two constitutionally recognized official languages and thousands of dialects, people of all religious beliefs, pockets of grinding poverty juxtaposed with unabated opulence and grandeur, India's Hindu roots have given the country the ability to coalesce as a country despite all the differences. The five-thousand-year-old ancestral faith has a tradition of generally promoting tolerance and advocating the concept of live and let live.

Even though at least eight out of ten Indians are Hindus, in 2006, the president of the country was a Muslim, the prime minister of India's

Parliamentary political system was a Sikh, the leader of the ruling party was an Italian Christian, and the leader of the Opposition was an Indian Christian. It is similar to having a Hindu as the president of the United States, a Buddhist as the leader of the House, and a Muslim as the leader of the Senate in a country where nearly eight out of ten people are Christians.

Even the staunchest Hindu parents in India and Nepal generally have no qualms about sending their children to Jesuit schools. The daily Christian prayers do not bother them as long as their children get the best education at the school.

As mentioned earlier, ancient Hindus believed in the superiority of the intellectual aspect of a person over his or her other traits. Even today, Hindu parents constantly remind their children of the importance of education and intellectual growth. It is not unusual to see Hindu children in the West excel in their studies.

The Western media coverage of Mother Teresa's death in India also captured the level of tolerance that Hindus maintain for other faiths. According to the media, "Mother Teresa went into the heartland of Hinduism, witnessed for Christianity, gained converts—and was seen by Hindu priests and commoner alike not as a threat but as an exemplar. The tears and wails of the crowds in Calcutta upon learning of her death on September 5 [1997] showed the depth of their adulation, and India's decision to give her a state funeral underscored it. How could Hindu believers respond so magnanimously to her Catholic mission in their midst? That they did says as much about the nature of Hinduism as it does about the gentle example of Mother Teresa."[146]

However, not all Hindus show the same level of tolerance to their brethren as they showed to Mother Teresa. Like the rest of humanity, Hindus also have their share of the good, the bad, and the ugly. History shows that religion can be a source of great good or terrible injustice; it all depends on how one uses it.

As history shows, from the beginning of time the leaders around the world have understood the power of religion, which provides a ready-made constituency of a group of people who have similar values, beliefs, and convictions. Opportunistic leaders are always looking for issues that resonate with a particular constituency. If they can find one, they can rally that constituency to grab power, garner prestige, or make money.

As with any other faith, Hinduism is not above exploitation by opportunistic leaders for political or financial gain. Sometimes the leaders exploit the communal conflicts by painting them with religious overtones. Although Buddha, a Hindu prince in real life, who would have inherited the kingdom, renounced political power and fame to teach others the path to end suffering, many leaders today deliberately inflame communal suffering for political power and fame.

Hindus also have their share of the charlatans who go around as spiritual gurus, and the unscrupulous even within the temples such as the leaders who grossly mismanage temple funds for personal gain, and priests (mostly at the holy sites on the Gangetic plain) who aggressively and incessantly pester the pilgrims for bigger donations.

***

Even today, over 98 percent of Hindus live in the Indian subcontinent. Normally, Hindus prefer to keep their *dharma* private and personal.

Although Hinduism had spread to Southeast Asia as early as the second century B.C., it did not appear in the West in any significant way until the early nineteenth century A.D. when Hindus started to migrate worldwide. Because many of the newly freed slaves in the British Empire refused to work on the plantations for their former masters, the British who ruled over India at the time permitted the plantation owners in their empire to recruit Indians. Many plantation owners in places such as Trinidad and Tobago, Fiji, Guyana, and Mauritius recruited the Indians who were mostly Hindus. Today, Hindus constitute a sizable portion of the populations of these countries.

Hinduism got its first major exposure in the West when Swami Vivekananda talked about the faith at the gathering of the World Parliament of Religions in Chicago in 1893. Before that, only a few select Western intellectuals such as Henry David Thoreau and Ralph Waldo Emerson had some understanding of the faith. Thoreau even mentioned that he was impressed with the "civility, intellectual refinement and subtlety" of the philosophy of Hindus.[147]

In the early twentieth century, a professor and a great Hindu scholar, Dr. Radhakrishnan, who later became the president of India, gave the world a fresh perspective on Hinduism through his books and lectures. Mahatma Gandhi introduced *ahimsa* and Karma Yoga to the world.

Over the last several decades, the West has been exposed to the various aspects of Hinduism. Several gurus opened their *ashrams,* "resting places," in the United States, promising spiritual enlightenment, and they attracted a large following.[148]

In the 1960s, the Beatles dabbled with Maharishi Mahesh Yogi's transcendental meditation. Followers of the International Society of Krishna Consciousness (ISKCON) started to build temples. A professor of philosophy turned mystic, guru, and philosopher calling himself Bhagwan Shree Rajneesh during the 1970s and 1980s and taking the name Osho in 1989, received media attention for his fleet of Rolls-Royce automobiles presented by his disciples.

Reportedly, some gurus even misused the trust placed in them.[149]

A new generation of Hindu gurus, often in their saffron-colored robes, long hair, and unkempt beards, continues to attract new disciples in the West. The trademark hair, beard, robe, and frequent chanting of *slokas* in Sanskrit appear to give the gurus an instant credibility. "Guru" in Sanskrit means "one who dispels the darkness."[150]

Except for Yoga, many in the West still do not know much about Hinduism. Paramhansa Yogananda was probably the first Yoga master of India to permanently live in the West and teach his non-sectarian and universal spiritual message based on Hinduism.[151] He came to the United States in 1920 and taught for nearly thirty years. The foundation he set up continues to "advocate cultural and spiritual understanding between East and West, and the exchange of their finest distinctive features."[152]

Without explicitly acknowledging Hinduism, some motivational speakers and authors in the United States have taken the spiritual elements of Hinduism and packaged them with other ideas, faiths, or beliefs. As a result, in the last few decades, many in the West may have been exposed to the elements of Hinduism without being fully aware of it.

***

Yoga has gained a universal recognition. Its ability to decrease stress has led many in the medical community in the United States to endorse its practice. Researchers have found that Yoga meditation stimulates the parasympathetic nervous system, which slows the heart rate and lowers blood pressure. Researchers also believe that meditation can grow neurons in areas of the brain involved in learning, memory, emotions, and awareness.

Some educational institutions are introducing Yoga to teach mindfulness to students who are overwhelmed by multi-tasking. Students are encouraged to tune out distractions, focus on what is happening in the present moment, and analyze emotions arising within them so that they can react to a situation skillfully with clarity and calm.

Reportedly, many computer programmers in the Silicon Valley are practicing Yoga to develop inner joy while succeeding at work. Supposedly, they are learning the skills to train their thoughts to perceive the challenging work and the hours they spend at it as a thing of joy!

Some businesses are using Yoga to attract new customers.[153] Despite an earlier reservation from its leaders, even some churches are using Yoga.[154]

The global proliferation of Yoga has benefited millions of people around the world. Yoga's *asanas* and *pranayama* have improved the quality of life for many.

Entrepreneurs are cashing in on the popularity of Yoga; some have copyrighted their techniques. Many Hindus object to the United States' granting of copyright protection to Yoga techniques that have been in the public domain for thousands of years.

Yoga's worldwide popularity has also prompted some individuals or groups to wrap Yoga around esoteric philosophical beliefs based on unique interpretations of elements of major religions and prevailing myths. Most of these individuals or groups have an uncanny knack for stringing together well-known words and phrases from the different faiths in such a way that it actually sounds like something intelligible is being said. Sometimes, they even include quantum physics.

Most of them are only commercially motivated and looking to sell their so-called "intensive" Yoga seminars, relaxation techniques, books, compact discs, and other paraphernalia. Unfortunately, reportedly, one group called Aum Shinrikyo exploited Yoga's popularity to create mayhem.[155]

Although Yoga is an intrinsic part of Hinduism and has been at its core for thousands of years, it is still a means or a tool to get to inner peace. One does not need to be subservient to a leader or to belong to an exclusive group. Nor does one need esoteric philosophical indoctrinations or need to drain one's bank balances to use Yoga's *asanas*, *pranayama*, and meditation techniques to change the way one conducts one's life, subdues one's ego, manages stress, and works toward inner peace.

***

The flexibility and the openness to accept new spiritual truths, while following the age-old traditions and teachings of the great seers and sages, are some of the greatest strengths of Hinduism.

As mentioned earlier, Indologists generally believe that the Hindu traditions have produced hundreds of thousands of texts in a wide variety of languages, most of which lie unstudied and effectively unknown.

Increasing global visibility of the Hindus will likely generate additional worldwide interest in Hinduism. This may prompt scholars, researchers, and scientists to explore the truths that lie unstudied and effectively unknown in many of these texts. I hope the new knowledge and the scientific truths discovered will further enrich the *dharma*.

9

HINDUISM AND SCIENCE

Human beings, vegetables or cosmic dust, we all dance to a mysterious time, intoned in the distance by an invisible player.
—Albert Einstein

In the West, religion and science have been at opposite ends for centuries. While faith is a virtue in religion, science relies on reason and evidence. Even today, issues such as creationism versus evolution and use of embryonic cells for medical research create a lot of passion on both sides. Church leaders and many faithful believe that the Holy Bible contains the absolute truth, and conflicts arise when science cannot support some long-held religious beliefs.[156]

In medieval times, the Vatican instituted the Inquisition to eradicate heresies such as views that contradicted the teachings of the Holy Bible. Giordano Bruno burned at the stake in 1600 for heresy—for not recanting that the Earth was not the center of the universe and publicly defending Copernicus, who had intentionally delayed publishing his position until the year of his natural death.[157] According to Papal orders, no blood could be shed in the method of death, because Jesus shed blood during the Crucifixion. Hence, Bruno burned alive so that no drop of blood was shed.

Galileo, often called "the Father of Modern Science," who along with Bruno supported Copernicus, missed burning at the stake only because he recanted. He was imprisoned for the rest of his natural life.

In the fourth century B.C., Aristotle stated that the Earth was stationary and at the center of the universe with the Sun, the Moon, the
planets, and the stars moving in circular orbits around it. Around A.D.
150, Ptolemy declared that the Earth stood still at the center of the universe and the stars moved around it in complicated orbits, like wheels
on wheels.[158] Physicists Stephen Hawking and Leonard Mlodinow write,
"Ptolemy's model of cosmos was adopted by the Catholic Church and
held as official doctrine for fourteen hundred years."[159]

Hawking and Mlodinow add, "According to the Old Testament, God
created Adam and Eve only six days into Creation. Bishop Ussher, pri-
mate of all Ireland from 1625 to 1656, placed the origin of the world
even more precisely [on the basis of Genesis and the ages of the generations starting with Adam], at nine in the morning on October 27, 4004
B.C."[160] The Bible says that the world was created in six days with light on
the first day and the Sun on the fourth day.[161]

Einstein's theories revolutionized the understanding of the universe. Using Einstein's theory, Belgian priest and astrophysicist Georges
Lemaitre came up with the "big bang theory" to explain the origins of
the universe. Scientists estimate that the universe is 13.7 billion years
old.[162] Radioactive dating proved that Earth has been around for nearly
4.6 billion years, and Charles Darwin concluded that the evolution of
the human species required millions of years. Scientists have confirmed
that the Sun is a gigantic fireball and the light is a byproduct of the thermonuclear reaction taking place in the Sun.

Whenever the scientific findings are inconsistent with the Biblical
text, the church leaders tend to pillory the scientists. The Vatican ac-
cused Einstein of "authentic atheism even if it is camouflaged as cosmic
pantheism."[163]

***

Hinduism has no conflict with science. Some Indian scientists even see
a consistency between modern science and the Vedic thoughts. For
example, based on his interpretations of the following passages from
the Rig Veda, nuclear scientist and astrophysicist Dr. Shri Ram Verma
contends that the Vedas had revealed some of these scientific truths a
long time ago:

The Earth not only takes round the Sun, but, along with it rolls round its own axis just like the wheel of a chariot, which rolls round on its axle and also runs on the road.[164]

The Sun sustained the Earth by its gravitational powers and stabilized, the heavenly region in the supportless space.[165]

The Moon is illumined by the Sun. It is not luminous by itself. The solar rays assume their seat in the Moon and make it illuminated.[166]

Researchers are also confirming that, nearly a thousand years before Galileo, Aryabhata, a Hindu scientist in the fifth century A.D., had calculated that the Earth revolved around the Sun.

Professor Wendy Doniger says, "Aryabhata ... was first to calculate the solar year accurately; he also made an explicit statement that the apparent westward motion of the stars is due to the spherical earth's rotation about its axis ..."[167]

Nobel laureate Amartya Sen adds, "Aryabhata's pioneering book, completed in 499 CE ... included ... an explanation of lunar and solar eclipses in terms respectively of the earth's shadow on the moon and the moon's obscuring of the sun, combined with methods of predicting the timing and duration of eclipses. ... [It included] an identification of the force of gravity to explain why objects are not thrown out as the earth rotates."[168]

In A.D. 662, Syrian astronomer-monk Severus Sebokht wrote, "I shall not now speak of the knowledge of the Hindus ... of their subtle discoveries in the science of astronomy ... of their rational system of mathematics, or of their method of calculation which no words can praise strongly enough ..."[169]

***

Hindus perceive the Supreme Soul as the *Om tat sat*, "*Om* that is the truth." Hence, science should ultimately be able to get to the same truth in a rational and logical manner.

Dr. Radhakrishnan says, "Science, philosophy and religion, all attempt to reveal the truth which is ultimately one and all-inclusive."[170] "[Swami] Vivekananda regarded modern science as a manifestation of the real religious spirit, for it sought to understand truth by sincere effort."[171]

Interestingly, Einstein also appeared to think along the same line as these great Hindu thinkers: "Science can only be created by those who are thoroughly imbued with the aspiration toward truth and understanding. The source of feeling, however, springs from the sphere of religion. To this there also belongs the faith in the possibility that the regulations valid for the world of existence are rational, that is, comprehensible to reason. I cannot conceive of a genuine scientist without that profound faith. The situation may be expressed by an image: science without religion is lame, religion without science is blind."[172]

***

It probably is easier for Hindus to be open to scientific inquiries because Hinduism has no authoritative book such as, for example, the Christians' Holy Bible, no one exclusive path to the Almighty, and no commandments directly from the Almighty. Hindus do have holy books written by the great *rishis* who were inspired by a higher power, but they are not the words of the Almighty. Hinduism does recommend paths to the Almighty but it says there may be even better paths.

Hinduism allows maximum flexibility in the pursuit of the Supreme. It asks the believers to find the "Truth" for themselves using any or all paths, which obviously includes science. Echoing Buddha's advice to his disciples, Swami Vivekananda says, "Believe nothing until you find it out for yourself."[173]

Just because the great thinkers of Hinduism promote rational scientific inquiries does not mean that all Hindus are comfortable with it. Similar to the Vatican and other religious leaders in the West, Hindus who have a stake in protecting the status quo believe one has the truths and that further investigation is futile.

Dr. Radhakrishnan writes, "Religion is not mere intellectual conformity or ceremonial piety; it is spiritual adventure. It is not theology but practice. To assume that we have discovered the final truth is the fatal error. The human mind is sadly crippled in its religious thinking by the belief that truth has been found, embodied, standardized and nothing remains for us to do except to reproduce feebly some precious features of an immutable perfection."[174]

Swami Vivekananda says, "Why religions should claim that they are not bound to abide by the standpoint of reason no one knows. ... If a religion is destroyed by such investigation [based on reason] it was nothing but a useless and unworthy superstition; the sooner it disappeared the better."[175]

If science irrefutably proves some belief of Hinduism wrong, then Hinduism will have to change. By further refining the *dharma*, and adding new spiritual truths, science can only enrich Hinduism.

Through decades of intense meditation and through the power of their mind, Hindu *rishis* of ancient times came up with various profound proclamations. They had no data or scientific facts to corroborate their declarations. In this chapter, we will look at a few of these precepts and see if modern science can affirm them.

THE UNIVERSE

It is almost impossible to imagine that more than three thousand years ago when almost everyone in the world believed that God created everything, the Sankhya and the Upanishad said Prakriti was responsible for the creation and the dissolution of the universe and everything in it. Moreover, the universe started from a mere potential and would dissolve into a mere potential again. Furthermore, according to the universal laws, the cycle will repeat itself forever as Gita 9.7 says, "During the Final Dissolution, all beings enter My Prakriti, and at the beginning of [next] cycle, I emit them again."

The Chandogya Upanishad describes how the world was non-existent, became existent, then became an egg; various parts of the egg became the features of the heavens and Earth.[176] This passage from the Upanishad must have confounded many until Lemaitre came up with his theory in 1927. Probably purely coincidentally, Lemaitre actually called his theory "the Cosmic Egg exploding at the moment of the creation."[177] Lemaitre's critic, the English astronomer and mathematician Fred Hoyle, possibly disparagingly coined the term "big bang theory" and it stuck.

Every day we are learning new things about our universe. Just a hundred years ago, people thought that the Milky Way galaxy was the extent of the universe. Today, scientists estimate that there are more than one hundred billion galaxies, some of them as far away as thirteen billion light years from Earth. The Milky Way itself is about 120 thousand light years across and contains more than one hundred billion stars

The speed of light is nearly 186,000 miles per second (300,000 km/ second). One light year, or the distance that is covered when traveling at the speed of light for a year, is nearly six trillion miles (nearly 9.5 trillion km). Thirteen billion years of travel time at the speed of light is an overwhelming distance, when one realizes that it takes light only eight minutes to get to Earth from the Sun and it takes light only 1.3 seconds to travel from Earth to the Moon.

However, a revelation that is even more fascinating is that all these billions of galaxies and all the hydrogen and helium that fuel all the stars, constitute only around 5 percent of the universe. The so-called "dark matter" and "dark energy," matter and energy that cannot be seen or easily detected, make up the remaining nearly 95 percent of the universe.

Astrophysicists theorize that some of the dark matter may be ordinary matter similar to the matter we see around us that comprise electrons, protons, and neutrons while most of it is made of exotic matter that we do not know yet. One of the dark matters the scientists have detected is the neutrino, which has an infinitesimal mass—one-tenth of a millionth of the mass of an electron. Neutrinos are called "ghost particles" because billions of them pass right through us every second without our even being aware of it.

Incidentally, ancient Hindus even before the time of Buddha recognized that air was not of infinite extension, and believed that a very subtle, uniform substance called *akasa* filled all space.[178] Although the literal translation of *akasa* is "sky," scholars had equated it with "ether" of pre-Einstein physics. Ancient Hindus' *akasa* appears to resemble dark matter and dark energy.

Current scientific belief is that the dark energy has no electric charge nor does it emit any visible or invisible radiomagnetic radiation for our instruments to detect its presence. However, it makes its presence known in a unique way.

Astrophysicists confirm the presence of the dark mass from its gravitational impact and from the number of positrons created when black matter particles collide. They attribute the stretching of the universe to the dark energy. It is acting as a repulsive force versus gravity, which is a force of contraction. Coincidentally, these forces appear similar to *rajas* and *tamas* at the Prakriti's universal scale as described earlier by the Sankhya *darshana*.

Astrophysicists also believe that the universe is stretching faster than the speed of light and is accelerating. If it keeps accelerating, astrophysicists believe that dark energy has the potential to rip every matter to basic elements of protons and electrons or even finer particles.

Astrophysicists call it the "big rip" when the dark energy tears the universe apart down to its essential building blocks. That will be the end of the universe as we know it; a universe ripped to shreds.

The inflation theory of how the universe came into existence appears to support what Hinduism has been saying for nearly three thousand years, that the universe started from mere potential. However, the big rip does not appear to support Hinduism's balancing of *rajas* and *tamas* resulting in *sattwa*.

Nevertheless, for some reason, if the dark energy's rate of acceleration slows down or if the dark energy value changes, the universe could collapse into a mere potential.

***

Cosmologists believe that stretching of the universe was actually decelerating until about 6.3 billion years ago.[179] Although there are some theories on why the stretching of the universe started to decelerate and why it is accelerating now, no one can predict that the stretching could not decelerate again.[180] It could slow down to such a level that its repulsive force's push balances out with gravity's pull, resulting in Hinduism's *sattwa*.

Even if the dark energy's rate of acceleration does not slow down, based on the current understanding of the universe, under one scenario, it is still possible for the forces to balance out and attain *sattwa*.

Astrophysicist Brian Greene wrote in *Newsweek*, "Einstein's equations show that if space contains ... not clumps of matter but an invisible energy, sort of like an invisible mist that's uniformly spread through space [such as the dark energy]—then the gravity exerted by the energy would be repulsive. ... [However] In universes whose dark-energy value is much smaller, the repulsive push changes to an attractive pull."[181]

If the stretching of the universe eventually alters the dark-energy value to a level at which the push changes to a pull, it will combine with gravity and instantly crunch the universe. Will the crunch again increase the dark-energy value and start the repulsive force? Will the strength of the repulsive force rise to a level where it balances with the force of gravity and results in the equilibrium of *rajas* and *tamas* that Hinduism talks about, leading to *sattwa* and the dissolution of the universe to a mere potential?

Speculating on how the universe will end may be premature as we know very little about the remaining 95 percent of our universe—the dark matter and dark energy. While it may be difficult to predict how the universe will end in 311 trillion years, science is getting closer to proving how the universe was created and, in the process, validating the spiritual intuition and the visions of the ancient Hindu *rishis*.

ALL FROM ONE

For thousands of years Hinduism has said that everything in the universe—stars, planets, humans, animals, plants, and all one can think of in this universe—originated from the same source, Prakriti. Having come from the same source, they are all connected.

Implying that most of the religions essentially based their beliefs on what they could observe or feel, a prominent self-proclaimed atheist, Michael Shermer, says, "Our brains evolved to connect the dots of our world into meaningful patterns that explain why things happen. These meaningful patterns become beliefs, and these beliefs shape our understanding of reality. Once beliefs are formed, the brain begins to look for and find confirmatory evidence in support of those beliefs, which adds an emotional boost of further confidence in the beliefs and thereby accelerates the process of reinforcing them, and round and round the process goes in a positive feedback loop of belief confirmation."[182]

So the question is, what dots did the Hindu *rishis* connect to conclude that a moth, a human, and the stars come from the same primordial source? How could these Hindu *rishis* of ancient times come to such conclusions, which only after nearly three thousand years appear to make sense? Besides the power of their mind, the *rishis* had no special tools. They did not conduct experiments nor did they arrive at these conclusions after elaborate mathematical computations. Maybe one day science will discover the parts of the human mind that can connect with another dimension and, possibly, find out how those *rishis* came to these profound conclusions.

In the last century, the pace of scientific advancement has accelerated. Today, finally, science is in a position to shed light on the three-thousand-year-old Hindu thinking.

***

The stars formed when the universe started to cool down after the big bang. All the stars, including the Sun, are giant fireballs caused by billions of hydrogen bombs exploding every second. In the hydrogen bomb, when the hydrogen fuses to helium, a small amount of mass is converted to energy, according to Einstein's famous equation, $E=mc^2$. This results in a tremendous amount of heat, light (photons), and electromagnetic radiation. The radiation exerts an outward pressure that balances the inward pull of gravity caused by the star's mass.

As fusion slows down with depleting levels of hydrogen, the counterbalancing forces of radiation diminish, allowing gravitation to compress the star inward. The contraction of the core causes its temperature to rise, and the temperature is high enough to fuse helium to make carbon and oxygen. Once all the nuclear fuel is exhausted, the outer layers of the star explode at more than a million miles per hour; the star sheds much of its mass. The remaining material at the core continues to collapse under its own gravity to a critical size or circumference, and can end up as a black hole. For Earth to turn into a black hole, it would have to compress to the size of a golf ball.

At the center of the black hole, the gravity is so intense that it creates an area known as the event horizon, the boundary from which even light cannot escape. Now we are learning that a black hole resides at the center of every galaxy, and the galaxies remain intact only because of the black holes.

The black hole in our Milky Way, which is estimated to have four million times the mass of the Sun, has an event horizon of about six million miles (9.6 million km). However, it pales in front of galaxy NGC 4889 in the Coma Constellation, which is supposed to have a black hole with the mass of nearly twenty-one billion Suns with an event horizon of forty-two billion miles. Incidentally, the distance from the Sun to Earth is only ninety-three million miles (149.6 million km). Future discoveries may make even NGC 4889 appear puny.

Actually, "black hole," a term coined in 1969 by an American scientist, may be a misnomer. Matter that does not fall in flies off at nearly the speed of light as bright, superheated plasma jets. Hence, very bright lights surround a black hole. The immense disks of gas orbit many black holes at a safe distance from the event horizon. Similar to the remnants of an exploded star, these disks of gas help nurture the formation of new stars. A black hole, in addition to being a destroyer, is also a creator—Shiva and Brahma of the Hindu pantheon, and the creator of a bright world, the Hindu's Swarga Loka!

The 4.6-billion-year-old Sun and Earth emerged from the remnants of exploding stars. All the elements found on Earth including the oxygen we breathe, calcium in our bones, and iron in our blood all come from the remnants of exploding stars. Some of these elements have combined to form proteins, carbohydrates, and nutrients to sustain our physical bodies.

Essentially, the universe is a giant recycler. In the absolute sense, nothing is truly created or destroyed—it merely changes from one type of element or form to another, from one type of energy to another, from mass to energy, or from energy to mass. The elements of the universe create the physical body, which reverts to the basic elements when the physical body dies.

***

Today, science also confirms that our bodies are not unique; they share the same basic elements with all other living beings on Earth. Cosmologist Joel Primack says, "All known life on Earth speaks the same genetic language. From bacteria to trees and humans, we are all descended from a single ancestor and share the same kind of genetic material: DNA. Not only do all living cells use DNA to store genetic information, they all use essentially the same code for turning this information into proteins and living organisms. It is as if, instead of the thousands of different human languages, everything were written in the same alphabet using words with the same meaning."[183] Moreover, the function of a protein appears to be the same regardless of whether the protein is in humans, yeast, or E. coli bacteria.

Sections of DNA contain unique genes; no other section carries the same genes. Each gene contains the code necessary to make a certain protein. "DNA can encode vast amounts of information and preserve and pass it on through countless generations with hardly a mistake."[184]

Not only do we share DNA and proteins with other living beings, but we also have a symbiotic relationship with many of them. Our bodies have more than a hundred trillion microbial cells either on them or in them, which is nearly ten times more than the number of cells that make up the human body. These microbes or microorganisms include bacteria, viruses, and fungi. Trillions of these microbes in the human intestine are busy digesting food, producing vitamins, and warding off diseases.

***

Modern science confirms that while other living beings on Earth share the same genetic material with us, we share our common heritage with the Sun and the Earth. The remnants from the explosions of the stars created the Sun, the Earth, and us, and we can trace the origins of the stars to the "big bang." Just as the ancient Hindu *rishis* realized after years of deep meditation, all of us in this universe did originate from the same primordial source, and hence, we are all connected.

TIME IS RELATIVE

Gita 8.18 says, "All living beings emanate from the Unmanifest at the coming of the cosmic day; at the cosmic nightfall, they go back into the Unmanifest."

Brahma's day and night, the cosmic day and the cosmic night, each last for 4.32 billion Earth years.[185] However, for the demigods who live on a different plane, their year is only 360 Earth years.

Through this precept that one cosmic day in the part of the universe where Brahma resides is billions of years for us, and a day for the demigods is about a year for us, the Hindu *rishis* of the ancient times declared that time is not constant throughout the universe or universes. It boggles the mind that the *rishis* could even conceive such radical concepts more than three thousand years ago.

***

Nothing in the universe is stationary. While it takes twenty-four hours for the Earth to turn on its axis and a year for us to orbit the Sun, it takes nearly 230 million years for our solar system to orbit the black hole at the center of our Milky Way galaxy.

The Earth rotates on its own axis at 1,040 miles per hour at the equator (1,670 km per hour). It orbits the Sun at 67,000 miles per hour (108,000 km per hour), and the Sun and the entire solar system orbit our black hole at 486,000 miles per hour (777,600 km per hour).

However, the stars close to the black hole are orbiting at millions of miles per hour.

Einstein showed that speed and gravitational force impact time. The tremendous time difference with Brahma's world can be scientifically possible, if Brahma's world were traveling extremely close to the speed of light or very close to the extreme gravitational force near the event horizon of a black hole. However, Brahma may not feel the speed just as we do not feel that we are hurtling through space at 486,000 miles per hour.

Incidentally, the prediction that all living beings on Earth will disappear at the end of Brahma's day or in 4.32 billion Earth years coincides with the depletion of fuel for thermonuclear reaction and the Sun turning into a red dwarf, thereby scorching the planet Earth.

MEDITATE TO INNER PEACE

Hindus believe that, among all living beings, only humans have the capability to connect with the Supreme Soul. It follows from this reasoning that inner peace opens the door to the Supreme Soul and, as the animals function mainly on instincts, only humans have the ability to meditate their way to inner peace. Can modern science support the assertion that, in the hierarchy of all living beings, only humans have the capability to attain inner peace?

***

Neuroscientist Dr. Jill Bolte Taylor says, "Although many of us think of ourselves as thinking creatures that feel, biologically we are feeling creatures that think." Our limbic system is the first one to react to the incoming sensory perceptions. Further, "… our limbic system functions throughout our lifetime, it does not mature. As a result, when our emotional 'buttons' are pushed, we retain the ability to react to incoming stimulation as though we were a two year old, even when we are adults."[186]

Dr. Taylor also says that our ability to process data about the external world starts at the level of sensory perception, which detects the information at the energy level. A complex set of neurons in our sensory systems processes the incoming neural code; cells along the way further define and refine the code until it reaches our limbic system.

The limbic system is the seat of fear and rage, which results in a fight or flight syndrome. The reaction from the limbic system is immediate and automatic. We share a similar limbic system with many other animals.

Scientists estimate that humans and chimpanzees share 99.4 percent of DNA, humans and mice share 90 percent, humans and nematode worms share 33 percent, and the human-to-human share is 99.9

percent.[187] Despite the 0.1 percent difference between humans, the probability of two people with identical DNA is one in ten billion.

While humans share 99.4 percent of their DNA with their nearest relative, the chimpanzees, and they both share a similar limbic system, the chimps barely have a frontal cortex. The 0.6 percent difference in the DNA is mostly the frontal cortex, the part of our mind where we think and make choices in a rational manner. The 0.6 percent difference in the DNA is huge because the difference between humans is only 0.1 percent.

Dr. Taylor says that the limbic system attaches a feeling to the incoming signal before it reaches the frontal cortex, which is the center for higher thinking. Dr. Taylor adds that our feelings will dominate unless we know how to engage our thinking brain. Unlike the animals with very limited or no cerebral cortex, humans have the ability to use the thinking brain. If we engage the thinking brain, the mind will flush out the automatic response of fear and rage from the limbic system, thus allowing us to make our own choices rather than having the limbic system drive them as in the case of many animals.[188]

Not only do we have the ability to override the limbic system inputs, but we can also learn the skills to train our thoughts. Based on the recordings of the brain activity of Buddhist monks who have spent a great deal of time meditating, scientists confirm that the adult brain is very malleable, and meditation can change the function of the brain in an enduring way.[189] Meditation can rewire the adult brain for more happiness, calm, and inner peace.

Among all living beings, only humans have the massive frontal cortex, which makes them the most likely candidates who can train their thoughts to overrule the inputs of fear and rage from the limbic system, and learn the skills to meditate their way to inner peace.

***

While modern science can support Hindus' belief that, in the hierarchy of all living beings, only humans have the capability to meditate and

attain inner peace, it is not advanced enough to scientifically examine
the link between the inner peace and the Supreme.

In the last hundred years, science has made great progress. Now we
know more about our universe such as the black holes, the dark energy,
and the dark matter. We also know more about our physical body such
as the genes, DNA, and stem cells.

We have started to harvest human organs and other body parts in
laboratories, which further validates the Hindu thinking that our bodies
stem from the elements of the universe. Now we also know that our body
is a giant molecular assembler and a disassembler. The DNA molecules
guide the actions of ribosomes to take apart the proteins and amino acid
molecules in our food and reassemble them to build our bodies.[190]

Even though science has made significant advances in many areas
and we know a lot more about the human brain and the neurological
mysteries than we did a century ago, we know very little about the functioning of our mind. We do not know if our mind is nothing but the
product of the synapses between the nearly eighty-six billion neurons or
a massively powerful organic quantum computer in which our thoughts,
feelings, new learning, and interpretations can rewrite the codes in qu-
bits. We do not know how we think what we think and why we think it.

Scientific investigation of the physical world, while very challenging,
may be comparatively less daunting than scientifically researching the
human mind and finding out what keeps us alive. Scientists have made
some inroads into unraveling the mysteries of the brain by attaching
electrodes onto the scalp to study brain waves, by injecting chemicals
and observing the flow through some form of imaging technique, and by
dissecting animal brains to study the correlation with humans. However,
experimenting with a fully functioning human brain can be physically,
ethically, and morally challenging. So far, we have isolated parts of the
physical brain responsible for the various functions of the body, and scientists plan to map the brain, but we know very little about our mind.

The advancing scientific knowledge will eventually lead us to a better understanding of all the mysteries of the mind, the mysteries of the
universe including the dark matter and dark energy, and the ultimate

truths. As Buddha says, "Three things cannot be long hidden: the Sun, the Moon, and the Truth."

Although we may be centuries away from scientifically proving that inner peace opens the door to the Supreme, there is no doubt that attaining inner peace will make our lives on Earth more pleasant, calmer, and possibly, happier.

10

HINDUISM AND OTHER FAITHS

Through ignorance a common man considers his own religion to be the best and makes much useless clamor; but when his mind is illuminated by true knowledge, all sectarian quarrels disappear.

—*Ramakrishna Paramahamsa*

The time from the seventh to the fifth century B.C. was a time of great spiritual revival in Asia. While Daoism (also interchangeably referred to as Taoism) and Confucianism were making inroads in China, around the same time Buddhism and Jainism rose up in the Indian subcontinent.

Besides exploring the common elements between the major faiths that rose up in the Indian subcontinent, this chapter also explores the common thread that connects Hinduism with Christianity.

BUDDHISM

Siddhartha Gautama, the future Buddha, was born a prince in Lumbini, an area that currently lies within the southern borders of modern-day Nepal. Apparently, after being born the future Buddha miraculously stood upright, took seven steps, and said, "This is my last birth—henceforth there is no more birth for me."[191]

Siddhartha lost his mother, Queen Maya, shortly after his birth, and the queen's sister Prajapati became his de facto mother.[192] Because she embraced Buddhism and played a significant role in the spread of Buddhism, many Buddhists regard Prajapati as the mother of Buddhism. Siddhartha, which means "every wish fulfilled," grew up in the luxuries of the palace. At the age of sixteen, Siddhartha married Yasodhara, a cousin, and had a son, Rahul.

Having been told by the astrologers that Siddhartha could conquer whatever he wanted, his father, King Suddhodhana, had great visions of his son conquering the sixteen or so other kingdoms and becoming the future emperor of India.[193] King Suddhodhana did not want any distraction to sway the young prince from his visions of greatness, and as such, had discouraged the prince from going out of the palace. He had made sure the young prince had access to every imaginable creature comfort and endless entertainment.

Siddhartha did go outside the palace four times and what he witnessed profoundly affected him. The first time, he saw an old person, the second time a sick person, and the third time a corpse. On the fourth visit outside the palace, he saw a holy man on his way to find an escape from the rebirth. Having recognized the impermanence of power, pleasure, prestige, and fame, he realized that this was his fate too, and the only way he could escape from the suffering of old age, sickness, and death was by escaping rebirth. Siddhartha also decided to find the path to escape from the rebirth. At the age of twenty-nine, he left the palace in the middle of the night, leaving all the creature comforts behind.

After having gone through many trials and errors, including living as an ascetic—punishing the body with extreme deprivation—at the age of thirty-five he sat under a tree in Bodhgaya. He began his meditation and his quest for the path to *nirvana.*

As the story goes, Mara, the evil one with demonic forces, was determined to distract Siddhartha from achieving *nirvana.* Mara sent his daughters to tempt Siddhartha with lustful dances, and taunt him with words to arouse his ego and pride. He sent monsters to arouse fear, create confusion, and undermine Siddhartha's efforts.

Mara failed. After forty-nine days, awakening came to Siddhartha. He saw all things as being impermanent and ever changing. Siddhartha

Gautama attained *nirvana* and became Gautama Buddha, the Awakened One.

Buddha gave his first sermon in Sarnath. He spent his life spreading the message of *nirvana* and died in Kushinagar at the age of eighty. Bodhgaya, Sarnath, and Kushinagar are places in northern India, close to the southern borders of Nepal.

Although some historians place his birth at 567 B.C. and his death at 487 B.C., based on the Buddha Nirvana Calendar and the start of the Buddhist era, it is very likely that Buddha was born in 579 B.C. and died in 499 B.C. The Buddha Nirvana Calendar, which is presumed to be based on the year of Buddha's nirvana, is 544 years older than the Gregorian calendar.[194] Buddha attained *nirvana* at the age of thirty-five and *parinirvana* at the age of eighty.[195] *Parinirvana* is the death of the physical body of a person who has already attained *nirvana*.

***

After twenty-nine years of palace luxuries and the extremes of sensory indulgences added to the six years of extremes of self-mortification and deprivation as an ascetic, Buddha advocated a middle way—a balance between the two extremes. Having said, "The world is filled with pain and sorrow but I have found a serenity that you can find too," Buddha in a very logical manner listed the following four noble truths:

1. Life is *dukkha*—"suffering, anguish."
2. The cause of *dukkha* is *tanha*—"craving, desire."
3. Eliminating the *tanha* will end *dukkha*.
4. The eightfold path will eliminate the *tanha* and lead to *nirvana*.

Greed and egos drive one's desires; the cravings for sensual pleasures, success, and wealth can be insatiable. Only moral and mental disciplines can eradicate *tanhas* and lead to *nirvana*.

Buddha characterized *nirvana* as *shunyata*, which some have defined as "emptiness," "total annihilation," "the extinction of existence, or flameout." Actually, *shunyata* means "a state of utmost tranquility, total silence, absolute peace, and quiet, or total serenity."

Buddha told his disciples to find the inner strength within themselves and diligently work out their own liberation. Instead of grace, Buddha advocates self-development. The following eight steps are the paths to *nirvana*:

1. Right understanding: To attain *nirvana*, one must grasp the four noble truths and control the desires that bind one to this *sansaar* for eternity, resulting in endless cycles of rebirth. As mentioned earlier, *sansaar* is the world of a continuous cycle of life followed by death. While the desires to do good and be like Buddha lead one toward *nirvana*, pursuing insatiable desires of sensual and materialistic pleasures fueled by greed and egos will only lead to *dukkha* and endless cycles of rebirth.

   Buddha asks one to face the desires and shortcomings, and compassionately face one's fears, including the fear of death. Moreover, recognizing death as an inevitable part of life helps one lead a more purposeful life.

2. Right thoughts: A person must genuinely work on controlling negative thoughts and feelings. Buddha says, "All that we are is the result of what we have thought. The mind is everything. What we think, we become."[196] Buddha wants one to think unselfishly and compassionately, approach things with a beginner's mind or without any preconceived notions, judgments, or expectations.

3. Right speech: It includes telling the truth and speaking in a way that is helpful while refraining from slander, malicious words, cursing, boasting, and raising one's voice. The Dharmapada, which is the Buddhist religious text, says, "Better than a thousand useless words is one single word that brings peace."[197]

4. Right conduct: Buddha taught that compassion and kindness are the most important qualities for a person to have. Rather than seek God's grace, Buddhism

wants one to show one's grace to others through compassion. Buddha wants one to control one's ego and develop *bodhiridaya,* "heart of enlightenment, love, and understanding." Love, compassion, tolerance, honesty, peacemaking, and thoughtfulness in everything one does are encouraged, but stealing, taking life, violence, cheating, and destruction of life or property are frowned upon.

Buddhism regards greed, hatred, and ignorance as three poisons. The Dharmapada says, "For hatred does not cease by hatred; hatred ceases by love; this is an old rule."[198] It adds, "Conquer the anger of others by non-anger, the evil with good; conquer the greedy by liberality, the falsehood by truth."[199] However, the Dharmapada also says, "Self conquest is indeed far better than the conquest of others."[200]

5. Right livelihood: It includes doing work that is useful without damaging people or the environment. Buddhism's five precepts for right livelihood are do not destroy life, steal, commit sexual misconduct, lie, or take intoxicating drinks. However, Buddhism does make an allowance for the person's intent and motives. For example, stealing could be forgiven if a person has to resort to stealing as the final desperate measure to feed a hungry child.

    As with Hinduism, right livelihood involves enjoying what the world has to offer without attaching oneself to it.

6. Right effort: One must cultivate self-knowledge and self-discipline, strive to be content and peaceful, and to encourage everything that is good, and make an effort to live wisely. The saying often attributed to Buddha is, "The secret of health for both mind and body is not to mourn for the past, not to worry about the future, but to live the present moment wisely and earnestly." Live every day as if it were the last day on Earth.

7. Right mindfulness: One should not do anything or behave in such a way that one regrets afterward. Mindfulness involves maintaining an awareness of everything life has to offer.
8. Right meditation: Meditation that gets rid of the ego, and quiets the mind, leading to the state of *anatta*, "no Self," and *nirvana*.

Actually, the eight paths can be grouped into three major groups as follows:

Wisdom: right understanding, right thought
Morality: right speech, right conduct, right livelihood
Mental discipline: right effort, right mindfulness, right meditation

***

In addition to the four noble truths, Buddha encouraged his followers to develop the following four attitudes:

Maitri:	Friendship and loving kindness toward others (*Metta* in Pali, a language possibly spoken in the region where the early followers compiled Buddha's teachings)
Karuna:	Compassion and to feel others' pain
Mudita:	Find joy in others' happiness (instead of envy and jealousy)
Upeksha:	Ability to remain peaceful and calm in any crisis, equanimity (also spelled *Upeksa, Upekka* in Pali)

These four qualities are also known as the Brahma Viharas or the Brahma's abodes. Besides developing these attitudes, later generations of Buddhists added the following five moral codes of conduct or *panchasila*, "five moral principles":

- *Ahimsa*
- Not to take what has not been given willingly
- No misconduct of senses such as sexual misconduct
- Abstain from lies, offensive remarks, or gestures
- Refrain from taking intoxicants that affect the mind such as drugs and alcohol

***

Although many authors depict young Siddhartha's luxurious palace life as a life of excesses and sensual entertainments, actually young Siddhartha's life must have revolved around the palace tutors and getting ready for his responsibilities—to be the future emperor of India. However, witnessing the old, the sick, and the corpse made him confront his ultimate fate. Very likely, when Siddhartha left the palace, he was seeking the path to inner peace.

That is what he accomplished. Through his awakening, Buddha showed the path to *nirvana*—a state of utmost tranquility, total silence, absolute peace and quiet, or total serenity.

Dr. Radhakrishnan says that Buddha was born a Hindu and died a Hindu. He adds, "While Buddha agreed with the faith he inherited on the fundamentals of metaphysics and ethics, he protested against certain practices which were in vogue at the time. He refused to acquiesce in the Vedic ceremonialism. When he was asked to perform some of these rites, he said: 'And as for your saying that for the sake of *dharma* I should carry out the sacrificial ceremonies [sacrificing an animal], which are customary in my family and, which bring the desired fruit, I do not approve of sacrifices for I do not care for happiness which is sought at the price of other's suffering.'"[201]

Buddha accepted the Sankhya and Upanishadic *darshanas* that, rather than the priestly rituals, attaining inner peace would release the faithful from the cycle of rebirth. Hence, when he found the path to *nirvana*, he believed he had found a path to freedom from the cycle of rebirth.

However, in areas such as the nature of the soul and the Supreme Soul, where the Sankhya and Upanishadic *darshanas* differed, Buddha withheld judgment. He refrained from endorsing either view. Reportedly, when asked about his views on the Supreme reality, Buddha refused to speculate on the nature of the transcendental reality.[202] Hence, Buddha called the state of inner peace and tranquility *nirvana* instead of adopting the Upanishadic term *moksha*.

Buddha was opposed to all those who had set views. He believed that if one adopts definite views, one gets concerned about defending them, which can lead to disputations with rival doctrines, resulting in pride. Having no view to defend, no prejudice to plead, one is free from doctrinarism. Buddha insisted that his followers should concentrate on the way leading to enlightenment.[203]

Buddha relied on logical reasoning and experience. He did not ask the faithful to accept anything on authority. Buddha's words were, "One must not accept my law from reverence, but first try it as gold is tried by fire."[204]

After the awakening, Buddha dedicated the rest of his life to teaching others. The Sutras and Pitakas are collections of Buddhist teachings. Pitaka means "basket." The faithful refer to the teachings as Buddhist *dharma*.

Even in his old age, Buddha was not interested in discussing metaphysical questions or the nature of the transcendental reality. He concentrated on issues that had an immediate bearing on the practical lives—issues that were under one's own individual control, which one could change to attain *nirvana*. To those who spoke about God, Buddha asked them to become pure and good like their God. Buddha's message was one of universal benevolence.

Buddhists regard the Buddha, the *dharma*, and the Sangha as the Three Jewels of Buddhism. Sangha means "community." To become a Buddhist, one takes an oath to follow the Three Jewels.

***

Shortly after Buddha's death, his disciples held the first councils of *arhats*. An *arhat*, "a worthy one," is someone who has absorbed all the teachings of Buddha and is enlightened, being free from *tanha*. During the first council, the *arhats* recited all the teachings to make sure they captured them correctly. The second council took place a century later. In the third century B.C., Emperor Ashoka called the third council during his reign.

Ashoka was the emperor of India, a land that extended from modern-day Pakistan and Afghanistan in the west to Assam and Bangladesh in the east and from the Himalayas on the north to near the current city of Bangalore in the south. He reigned for forty-one years until his death in 232 B.C.

Ashoka achieved what King Suddhodhana wanted of the young prince Siddhartha—military conquests over the many kingdoms and to be the emperor of India. The last battle Ashoka fought and won was the fierce battle for the kingdom of Kalinga. Upon seeing an unimaginable loss of lives, with more than a hundred thousand dead, the river of blood, and the wailing relatives of the dead, a sense of revulsion came over the emperor. He proclaimed *ahimsa* and decided to follow Buddha's teachings.

Maybe Emperor Ashoka saw the wisdom in young Siddhartha's escape from the palace—to find a way to end the suffering rather than to create one. As mentioned earlier, *ahimsa* means non-violence in words, deeds, and thoughts.

Ashoka was a Hindu emperor. The emperor's embracing of Buddha's teaching gave it a distinct identity. Ashoka dedicated the rest of his life to spreading the message of Buddha. He sent his son and daughter to neighboring countries, and dispatched groups of messengers around the world.

Under Hinduism, even an emperor may not impose his religious belief on others. Besides, Ashoka had no intent to compel his subjects or anyone to follow Buddha's teachings. He preached religious tolerance to such an extent that he decided to chisel his edicts on rocks. Following are some examples of his Rock Edicts:

> One who reverences one's own religion and disparages that of another from devotion to one's own religion and to glorify it over all other religions does injure one's own religion most certainly.[205]
>
> Do not quarrel about religions; concord is meritorious. Do not imagine that you have a complete hold on

Truth. You may not have it; no religion has a monopoly of Truth.[206]

Ashoka's embrace of Buddha's teachings invigorated Buddhism. The faith spread outside India. It was during Ashoka's time that King Devanampiya Tissa of Sri Lanka and many of his courtiers and subjects adopted the Buddhist *dharma*.

Buddha's message may have reached all the way to Greece and many parts of the Hellenic Empire (ca. 323–146 B.C.). In around A.D. 507, Afghans even carved the statues of Buddha on the sides of the cliff in Bamiyan, which the Taliban Muslims dynamited in 2001. With the advent of Christianity and Islam, Buddhism disappeared from all the areas that lie west of the borders of modern-day India. Buddhism prevails mostly in the areas that lie east, north, and south of the borders of modern-day India.

***

Buddha's early followers strived to be an *arhat*, preferring a monastic life focused on education and learning. They called it "the way" or "teaching of the elders"—Theravada.

Even though Buddha had declined to comment on the existence of the soul and the Supreme Soul, early Buddhist thinkers rejected their existence.[207]

Today followers primarily in Sri Lanka, Thailand, Mynamar (previously known as Burma), Laos, and Cambodia practice Theravada. Followers of Theravada regard Buddha as the pathfinder and believe that Buddha will reappear as Maitreya to reintroduce the teachings when people have forgotten them.

As Theravada was becoming increasingly monastic, some felt that the faith should become more accessible to the masses, as Buddha had done by travelling around the country and teaching the common folks. With the passage of time, differences of opinion arose among the followers of Buddhism.

Buddhism split into two schools—Mahayana and Theravada. Mahayana, "the great vehicle," became the newer school. It started in Northwest India and from there spread to the northern countries of Asia.[208]

Rather than following a monastic life spent on education and learning, Mahayana emphasized compassion and helping the needy. Some people even started to refer condescendingly to Theravada as Hinayana, "the little vehicle."

Mahayana believes in an Eternal Buddha, which is analogous to the Hindu concept of Paramatma or the Supreme Soul. They regard Gautama Buddha as the earthly incarnation of the Eternal Buddha. Today Mahayana is practiced in Vietnam, China, Korea, and Japan.

Vajrayana, or Tantric Buddhism, is a branch of Mahayana. Through mysticism and esoteric arts, it aims to attain *nirvana* in one lifetime rather than over successive lifetimes. Followers generally believe that by pronouncing the *mantra* in the correct manner, or by using the *yantra* in a special way, they will attain the highest bliss in the shortest time. Vajrayana prevails mostly in Nepal, Bhutan, Tibet, and Mongolia. A *yantra* is a symbol or an instrument to invoke astrological, spiritual or magical powers.

Mahayana believes in a *bodhisattva*, which is a combination of two words, *bodhi*, "enlightened," and *sattva* or *sattwa*, one of the *gunas* from Hinduism. While some see the *bodhisattva* as someone who is nearing *nirvana*, others perceive the *bodhisattva* as an enlightened *sattwika* who has attained *nirvana* but who has chosen to re-enter the cycle of *sansaar* to save other sentient beings.

An *arhat* seeks his *nirvana*, and a *bodhisattva* seeks *nirvana* for others. Theravada does not recognize the concept of *bodhisattva*.

Normally when Buddha is shown next to a *bodhisattva* in Indian sculptures of the second and third centuries A.D., Buddha is shown with no ornaments; a *bodhisattva* will be adorned in princely attire with ornaments and a halo. The attire reflects the *bodhisattva's* choice to remain in the worldly realm full of passion and material desires, but his halo reminds one of his *nirvana*.

Mahayana regards Manjushri as the *bodhisattva* of wisdom. In one hand, he carries the sacred text of wisdom and in the other a sword to cut through the illusion to get to the truth.

Avalokiteshwara is the *bodhisattva* of perfect compassion, who can appear on Earth in either a male or a female form. As a female, she is infinitely merciful and comes to help all those who need her and call on her. She is worshipped as Kuan-yin in China and Taiwan, Kannon in

Japan, and Tara in Tibet, Nepal, and India. Tibetan Buddhists venerate
the Dalai Lamas as the compassionate male *bodhisattva* Avalokiteshwara.

While the followers of Theravada use scriptures written in Pali, followers of Mahayana use scriptures written in Sanskrit. Historians believe that
Sanskrit may have been the language commonly used in the areas where
the Mahayana started, whereas Pali may have been the language commonly used in the region where Buddha's early followers finalized Theravada.

***

Just like the great *rishis* of the Vedas and the various *darshanas* of
Hinduism, Gautama Buddha enriched Hinduism. Buddha brought
compassion, non-violence, respect for life, kindness to animals, and the
importance of seeking inner peace as advocated by the Upanishads to
the forefront of Hinduism. As mentioned earlier, Hindus regard Buddha
as the incarnation of Vishnu, an *avatar*, on a par with Rama and Krishna.
Hindus believe Buddha came to teach the faithful the right path of
living. The Gita considers *nirvana* the same as *ananda*, "eternal bliss."[209]

Hinduism is a collection of realizations of the spiritual truth.
Everything in Buddha's teaching could be reconciled with Hinduism.
Buddha addressed the specific issue of suffering, and his reluctance to
comment on the soul and the Supreme Soul allowed Hindus to maintain
the status quo. Hinduism embodied the Buddhist teachings.

For example, "For hatred does not cease by hatred" is a famous
teaching of Buddha, which is also the essence of the Mahabharata.[210]
The Gita, which was in the final form long after Buddha, shares similar teachings. The Gita's three gates to hell—desire, anger, and greed—
may have stemmed from Buddha's three poisons: greed, hatred, and
ignorance. The following passage from the Gita appears consistent with
Buddha's eightfold path:

> Non-violence, truthfulness, absence of anger, renuncia-
> tion, tranquility, aversion to fault finding, compassion for
> all creatures, modesty, steadiness, forgiveness, patience,
> and freedom from covetousness, malice and excessive
> pride—these are the marks of the one born of divine
> qualities. (Gita 16.2–3)

In the following Yoga Sutra, Patanjali Rishi shows how Buddha's Brahma Viharas, namely, *maitri, karuna, mudita* and *upeksha* can be the paths to inner peace:

> By cultivating an attitude of friendship [*mudita*] toward those who are happy, compassion [*karuna*] toward those in distress, joy [*mudita*] toward those who are virtuous, and equanimity [*upeksha*] toward those who are non-virtuous, lucidity arises in the mind.[211]

The Mandukya Upanishad and Buddha say that if attached to the source of pleasure, one cannot escape pain and sorrow; both also agree that the chief cause of suffering is ignorance.[212]

Following the example of Sanghas set by the Buddhists, Adi Shankaracharya established four *maths*, "religious orders," in the four corners of India.[213]

Just as the Hindus recognized Buddha as one of the *avatars*, Theravada accepted some of the Hindu gods such as Brahma, Narayana (another name for Vishnu), Indra, and other deities. Even today, for example, the Buddhists in Thailand worship many of these divinities at the various shrines.

The Mahayana included some of the Hindu gods, for example, Vishnu is the Bodhisattva Padmapani, one of the Avalokiteshwaras.

As in Hinduism, Buddhism also uses symbols to convey a message. The story of Mara—the evil one with demonic forces, who was determined to distract Siddhartha from achieving *nirvana* by various means—was the Buddhists' way of showing human weaknesses. Actually, Mara was not the evil one with demonic forces; it was the mind. The various forces of distraction were lust, fear, pride, and doubt, all of which are within everyone. To awaken, one needs to overcome the forces of distraction. "The enemy we have to fight is within ourselves."[214]

Through symbols, the Buddhist "Wheel of Life" shows the right path to *nirvana*. A monkey jumping from tree to tree symbolizes the fleeting mind, a pregnant woman symbolizes procreation, a house with five windows symbolizes the five senses, a woman giving birth symbolizes the consequence of people's action, and a corpse symbolizes death. "Wheel of Life" is a popular Buddhist painting.

Similar to Hinduism, the lotus is the symbol of human life and enlightenment. The lotus with its roots in the mud manages to come out and bloom. While one's roots may be in lust, fear, pride, and doubt, one can still find enlightenment and attain *nirvana*.

***

It appears that the people in the East did not have the concept of exclusiveness when it came to the Supreme and were generally receptive to spiritual wisdom from the outside, and had a tradition of absorbing what was good in others.[215]

People in the East generally believed the different religions and teachings that evolved in the regions to be the different paths to the same God. Buddhism has coexisted with Confucianism, Daoism, and Shinto for more than two thousand years.[216]

In the sixth century B.C., Confucius stressed moral conduct, respect for learning and study, and kindness toward humanity as some of the most important qualities to develop. Confucius told his followers, "Do not do to others what you do not wish done to you." The Chinese built many Confucius temples from around 100 B.C., to show respect for the great teacher.

Daoism, founded by Lao-tzu in the sixth century B.C., taught the way to achieving immortality by seeking oneness with Dao (also interchangeably referred to as Tao) through chanting, physical exercise, and meditation. Daoism also believed that everything came out of Dao originally; it permeates everything, and eventually everything returns to Dao.

Shinto, the way of the gods, is the indigenous faith of the people of Japan. It believes that Kami, the invisible spirit beings, occupy and govern the natural world, and everything contains the sacred spiritual essence.

The sacred spiritual essence of Shinto, the essence that permeates everything in Daoism and Hinduism's divine essence may be the different human perceptions or interpretations of the same spiritual essence. Meditation is the gateway to these spiritual wisdoms.

Although China declared Buddhism as the state religion in A.D. 379, followers of Confucianism, Daoism, and Buddhism believed that "religions are many, reason is one; we are all brothers."[217] By the fourth century A.D., Buddhism also was widely practiced in Korea.

Buddhism has coexisted with Shinto in Japan since A.D. 593, when Prince Shotoku Taishi established it as the official religion of the imperial court.[218] Prince Shotoku perceived Shintoism, Confucianism, and Buddhism as complementary faiths.

Instead of tearing down the Shinto jinja, "shrine," the Buddhist missionaries in Japan built their temples nearby. They proclaimed that the Shinto's Kami and the *bodhisattvas* (*bosatsu* in Japanese) of Mahayana Buddhism were the same thing.[219]

Even today, many Buddhists in Japan often worship a range of gods from the Hindu pantheon. For example, goddess Saraswati is Benjaiten, who carries a Japanese lute instead of the Indian stringed instrument *veena*; goddess Lakshmi is Inari; and one of the celestial bodies, Bontenis, is generally associated with the Hindu god Brahma.

***

Unlike Christianity, for example, in which people from Jesus of Nazareth to Mother Mary to all the apostles have the same European facial features all over the world, Buddha's facial features differ from country to country. Each group perceives Buddha in its own image and as such, the statue of Buddha in Japan has different facial features from the ones in China, Thailand, Sri Lanka, or India.

Even today, most Japanese follow Buddhism and Shinto. Most Taiwanese follow Buddhism, Daoism, and Confucianism—all at the same time. Even though Buddha did not believe in rituals, his followers have managed to establish rituals to coalesce the community.

However, as in all religions, just because people follow the faith does not necessarily mean the faithful abide by the teachings. Notwithstanding the teachings against attachments to materialism, cravings, and so on, many Buddhists in the affluent parts of Asia hanker for everything with a designer label and the most prestigious name brands.

Despite the great focus on meditation, most Buddhists do not meditate. Similar to the *bhaktas* in Hinduism, many Buddhists worship Buddha as divine and hope Buddha's blessing will lead them to *nirvana*.

***

The Western world is getting more familiar with Buddhism. Nearly a hundred years ago, it started with Western intellectuals and organizations promoting meditation and imparting Buddhist teachings in Europe. The Chinese takeover of Tibet in 1959 and the attention the media paid to the Tibetan cause during the times of the Cold War exposed the West to Buddhism.

In Tibet, the country's ruler, the Dalai Lama (Ocean of Wisdom) was also its religious leader. Tibetans revered the Dalai Lama as the incarnation of compassionate Bodhisattva Avalokiteshwara.

Through an elaborate process, Tibetans determined that when the thirteenth Dalai Lama, Thubten Gyatso, died in 1933, he was reborn in the village of Takser in the body of Lhamo Thondup in 1935, fifth of sixteen children of a farming and horse-trading family. Lhamo Thondup became Tenzin Gyatso, the fourteenth Dalai Lama.

During the Chinese Communist invasion, many Tibetans lost their lives. The fourteenth Dalai Lama and his entourage fled to India and settled in Dharmasala, a small town in the foothills of the Himalayas in northern India. Because it was during the Cold War, which was a period of great political and military tension between the Western powers and the Communist world backed by the Soviet Union, the Dalai Lama became the poster child in the West for the Communists' atrocities for territorial ambitions.

Dressed as a monk, publicly the Dalai Lama advocated Tibet's liberation by peaceful means. He preached a message of compassion, peace, and harmony and became the face of Buddhism in the West. Hollywood celebrities such as Richard Gere embraced Buddhist teachings and became big supporters of the Dalai Lama's Tibetan freedom struggle.

Nearly five decades of the Dalai Lama's tireless effort to promote the Buddhist message of peace, compassion, mindfulness, and care for all living creatures have greatly bolstered the faith and gained new followers. Rather than seeking to convert people to Buddhism, the Dalai Lama seeks to make people more compassionate.

Incidentally, scientists confirm that humans have mirror neurons, which can make them physiologically susceptible to compassion. Neuroscientist Dr. V. S. Ramachandran says, "Anytime you watch someone doing something the neurons that your brain would use to do the same thing become active—as if you yourself were doing it. If you see a person being poked with a needle, your pain neurons fire away as though you were being poked."[220]

The Dalai Lama believes compassion is the foundation of a good heart, which acts out of a desire to help others. He adds that compassion toward others makes lives meaningful and is the source of all lasting happiness and joy.

By splitting the spiritual role from the head-of-state function, the Dalai Lama recently changed the fourteen-generation-old tradition and relinquished his political role as the head of the Tibetan government. He plans to spend the rest of his life as, in his words, "a simple monk" promoting the Buddhist message of compassion. Although the Dalai Lama may have failed in liberating Tibet from China, he greatly succeeded in spreading the essence of Buddhism around the world.

JAINISM

Nataputta Varadhamana, also called Mahavira or the great hero, was the last prophet of Jainism, or Jain Dharma. Even though the Jains believe that Jainism started centuries earlier and there were twenty-three prophets before Mahavira, scholars generally contend that Jainism might have started to crystallize by the ninth century B.C. Jains call their prophets *tirthankaras*, "the pathfinders." They believe that Rishabha was the first *tirthankara* and Mahavira was the last one. Jains also believe in *karma*, the cycle of rebirth, and *moksha*.

Similar to the *bodhisattvas* of Mahayana Buddhism, Jains believe that the *tirthankaras* are teachers who inspire and encourage others to free their soul by their own efforts. Jains revere Mahavira for being a *jina-*, "the victorious one," who conquered the lower passions and became free of attachments, and freed his soul. Mahavira Nirvana Samvat, which started in 527 B.C., commemorates Mahavira becoming a *jina*. Jains regard all the *tirthankaras* as *jinas*.

Jains believe that all living beings have souls and that to inflict harm on another soul is the biggest sin. Hence, some of them take the utmost precautions not to kill even the smallest insects. The concept of *ahimsa* is at the core of their faith. They regard *ahimsa* as *param dharma*. *Param* means "supreme."

Jains consider killing any person, no matter their crime, is unimaginably repugnant. They are strict vegetarians. Some Jains even extend the *ahimsa* concept to vegetables and plants and may curtail their consumption.

Jains normally do not pursue professions that may involve injury to living beings. For example, most of them do not engage in farming because of the potential of harming the insects. They are mostly in business and medical professions.

Mahavira, who was born in 599 B.C., was an elder contemporary of Gautama Buddha. However, unlike Buddha, who refrained from speculating on the nature of the Supreme Soul, the soul, and God, Mahavira appears to have views similar to the Sankhya *darshana*. Jains believe that natural laws govern the eternal universe. They do not believe in an omnipotent Supreme Being or a creator.

Jains believe in the soul and the freeing of the soul. Jains view God as the unchanging traits of the pure soul of each living being. Hence, similar to Sankhya, there could be as many gods as there are freed souls. One is responsible for freeing one's own soul.

Jains believe in heaven and hell. Actions have consequences. While good deeds lead to heaven, bad deeds lead to hell.

Mahavira took asceticism to new heights. Jains believe in controlling the desires of material possessions, fame, achievement, extreme lust, and sensuousness of the world.

Some see the Charvakas' insistence on pleasure seeking as a reaction to Jainism's emphasis on asceticism. As mentioned earlier, Charvakas believed that there was no god or afterlife, and promoted maximum materialistic and sensual pleasures in one's lifetime. Many consider Buddhism the middle way between these two diametrically opposed viewpoints.

Often the statues of Buddha and Mahavira look alike; both appear in meditative positions. Only upon close inspection, one can see the differences. Mahavira is most often depicted as naked or with clothes covering only his private parts. At the center of his chest, Mahavira has a Srivatsa, an auspicious Hindu emblem that resembles a flower or a diamond.

Jainism promotes rational perception, rational knowledge, and rational conduct. For the nearly four million Jains around the world, the festival of Diwali is a celebration of Mahavira becoming a *jina*.

Many credit Jainism for Mahatma Gandhi's stance on *ahimsa*. Various sects within Hinduism may have adopted vegetarianism due to strong Jain influences. Reflecting their compassion toward animals and all living creatures, Jains operate many animal shelters and bird sanctuaries in India.

SIKHISM

Centuries of Hindus and Muslims living next to each other led to the rise of inspirational leaders such as Kabir and Nanak in the fifteenth and sixteenth centuries A.D., who advocated non-sectarianism. In his later years, in 1582, even the powerful Muslim emperor Akbar formed a new faith that drew on the elements of both Hinduism and Islam; he called his new faith Din-e-Ilahi, "the Divine Faith."

Kabir, a Muslim, was greatly influenced by Hinduism and Sufism. In the thirteenth century A.D., the Persian poet and a renowned Sufi mystic, Jalal-ud-din Muhammad Rumi, preached, "All religions are in substance one and the same."[221]

Kabir accepted the Hindu concepts of *karma*, Brahman, *maya*, and *moksha*, and the Muslim concepts of one God with no *avatars*, no idol worship, and no caste system. He set aside the authority of the Vedas and the Koran, and opposed the zealots on both sides. He believed that God was present within us and not "out there." He saw no purpose in the empty rituals, prostrating in a mosque or temple, reciting holy books to no end or praying five times a day, and performing priestly rituals. He advocated that followers mentally focus on God by singing *kirtans* (hymns) with other *bhaktas*.

On the other hand, Nanak, a Hindu and a younger contemporary of Kabir, took elements from Islam and preached a message that was similar to that of Kabir. However, unlike Kabir, Nanak accepted the gods of the Hindu pantheon and tolerated rituals. He also regarded lust, anger, greed, materialism, and ego as the five obstacles to the path to *moksha*. Kabir called his god Rama, and Nanak called his god Hari. Nanak called his followers Sikhs, "the ones ready to learn," or "disciples." In turn, his disciples saw him as a teacher and called him Guru Nanak.

***

After Guru Nanak's death, the Sikhs named a new guru and maintained the tradition of teaching. The increasing numbers of Sikhs brought the group additional visibility and, consequently, additional scrutiny from the Muslim rulers of the time. The emperor ordered the Sikhs to convert to Islam. The gurus who defied the emperor's order were tortured and executed.

In 1604, the fifth guru, Arjan (also spelled Arjun), compiled Guru Granth Sahib, also known as the Adi Granth, a collection of hymns and teachings, by combining teachings of all the previous gurus with Guru Nanak's. Arjan also included other popular hymns of *bhakti* and Sufi saints of the time.

Emperor Jahangir tortured and executed Arjan in 1606. Newer gurus took his place and carried on with the teachings.

The late seventeenth century was a time of political instability on the Indian subcontinent. In 1699, the tenth guru, Govind, formally organized the Sikhs into a political and military force of *khalsa*, "the pure." He also maintained five insignias of the faith: uncut hair, a sword, shorts, an iron or steel wristband, and a comb.

Guru Govind was also a poet. As a part of his daily prayer, Mahatma Gandhi recited several verses from Guru Govind's composition.[222] Guru Govind also revised the Guru Granth Sahib to include one of his own hymns and the hymns of the ninth guru.

In 1708, Guru Govind was assassinated. However, before his death, the guru discontinued the line of succession and declared the religious text Guru Granth Sahib as the Sikhs' eleventh and final guru. Sikhs regard the Guru Granth Sahib as the living voice of all their gurus.

***

A Sikh's congregational worship centers on reading and recitation of the Guru Granth Sahib. It says that there is but one God and his name is Truth. He is the creator, who never dies and is beyond the cycle of birth and death. He was true in the beginning, and has ever been true; he is also true now. A Sikh aspires to move from a *manmukh*, "one attached to the worldly life," to a *gurmukh*, "one devoted to God," to the final stage of *sachkand*, "a blissful state beyond the continuous cycles of rebirth."

Harmandir Sahib, also known as the Golden Temple at Amritsar, India, is the Sikhs' holiest *gurudwara*, "the door to the guru" or the place of worship. Harmandir means "Hari temple."

Every *gurudwara* has a *langar*, "community kitchen," attached to it where volunteers prepare and serve simple food for free, mostly vegetarian, to anyone who comes to the *gurudwara*. The faith encourages selfless service. For nearly twenty-six million Sikhs around the world, the festival of Diwali is a celebration of the return of the sixth guru from captivity. Hola Mohalla is the Sikh version of the festival of Holi.

Except for Nanak's teachings, neither Emperor Akbar's Din-e-Ilahi nor Kabir's teachings became new religions. Sikhs revere Guru Nanak as their first guru and the founder of their faith. Sikhism is the last of the four prominent faiths that sprouted in the Indian subcontinent.

CHRISTIANITY

As mentioned in the Acknowledgement section of this book, about forty-five years ago, I promised myself to explore Christianity. In this section, after a brief synopsis of the faith, I touch on a couple of areas to explore the impact of different historical trajectories.

I find that despite the obvious outwardly differences, Christianity and Hinduism are not very different at the spiritual core.

***

Although today more people in the world identify themselves with Christianity than with any other religion, Christianity appears to have had a rather turbulent beginning.

For the first three hundred years after the Crucifixion, followers of Jesus even argued about who Jesus was and what his message was. Gospels written by different people over the three hundred years in the

name of various apostles were often in total conflict with each other.[223]
The proponents of some of the diverse views were:[224]

1. Ebionites, who believed that Jesus was the Jewish mes-
    siah, who was not divine at birth, but God allowed
    him to redeem humanity's sin through his sacrifice;

2. Marcionites, who believed that the Jewish God was
    full of wrath and impossibly strict, and Jesus came to
    free the Christians from the Jewish God;

3. Gnostics, who believed that Jesus had come to free us
    from suffering and focused on enlightenment, wis-
    dom, and gaining salvation through knowledge;

4. Thomasines, who believed that all of us have a spark
    of divinity within us, and Jesus showed us how to re-
    discover it.

If one were to substitute the word "God" for "Jesus," the last two views
above would appear consistent with Hinduism. Incidentally, Gnostic, derived from the Greek word "gnosis," means "knowledge" and appears
similar to the Sanskrit word *gyana*, which also means "knowledge."

After centuries of persecution, followers of Jesus eventually got a big
boost when the Roman emperor Constantine embraced Christianity.

According to *U.S. News & World Report*, "In 312, Constantine, one of
the four Caesars at the time, reputedly had a vision that led to his con-
version ... fighting under the insignia of the cross, Constantine defeated
his last rival to become the emperor of Rome in 324 and, having unified
the empire politically, he moved swiftly to do the same ecclesiastically."[225]

Scholar and writer Thomas Cahill writes, "But as he [Constantine]
looked closer at his chosen instrument of unity, the new emperor was
disgusted to learn that Christianity was itself riven by deep theological
divisions and the rigidity and mutual hatred that such divisions encourage. ... He was going to bring this nonsense to end—as a military man,
he called 'a universal council of bishops and force them into agreement,
of what sort he didn't care.'"[226]

Emperor Constantine convened the Council of Nicaea, where at
least two hundred and fifty bishops met to formulate articles of faith.

The council agreed on the Holy Trinity—the Father, the Son, and the Holy Ghost (also referred to as the Holy Spirit).

Jesus was the Son of God, the Father in the heavens. God was the creator, the source of all that is seen and unseen. Through Jesus, all things were created. The Holy Ghost was the spirit of life.

The religion had good and evil; God was good and Satan, the devil, was evil. The religion traced its basis to the origin of humanity, Adam and Eve, and their committing of sin by eating the forbidden fruit, a sin that Adam and Eve's progeny, the human race, bears for eternity. One is born a sinner; the only way for a human to achieve atonement from his or her sins is through Jesus Christ, his or her Lord.

Because of the virgin birth (Mother Mary having been impregnated by the Holy Ghost), Jesus was free from the stain on humanity of the sin of Adam and Eve.

In addition to original sin, Christians regard pride, envy, anger, sloth, gluttony, lust, and greed as the seven deadly sins. Christians believe that human beings are sinful and that sin is intrinsic to human nature. Christians want the faithful to confess their sins and return to Jesus for forgiveness.

They believe sin is the reason for death and suffering being part of the human story. The Bible says, "The wages of sin is death; but the gift of God is eternal life through Jesus Christ our Lord."[227]

However, eternal life does not occur until Jesus returns. Until that time, the dead are in a state of purgatory. When Jesus returns, he calls the dead from their graves. He groups them with the faithful who are still living. The saved ones will ascend to heaven with Jesus. Those who have not confessed their sins or followed Jesus will be damned and will burn in hell for eternity.

The bishops at the Council of Nicaea shaped Christianity and ensured a central role for the church. The faithful saw the pope as God's representative on Earth.

Professor of Religion at Princeton University Elaine Pagels says that the church labeled the gospels with opposing views as misguided teachings and ordered them destroyed.[228]

***

The New Testament was in its final form by around the end of the fourth century A.D. The gospels such as the Gospel of Matthew and the Gospel of John were immortalized.

Although the church had labeled the gospels with opposing views as misguided teachings and had ordered them destroyed, to the utter surprise of many historians, some opposing views were hidden for centuries and escaped destruction.[229] Existence of these gospels was unknown until the Gospel of Mary Magdalene was found in 1896 in Egypt. So far, this is the only known gospel written in the name of a woman.

In 1945, an additional forty-six scriptures, which included the Gospel of Thomas, were found also in Egypt near a place called Nag Hammadi. These findings dramatically changed the understanding of early gospels and the evolution of Christianity itself.

The Gospel of Mary and the Gospel of Thomas focus purely on Jesus' spiritual message. It was about awakening through the light shed by the inner wisdom.

According to Professor of Ecclesiastical History at Harvard University Karen L. King, "Gospel of Mary reproduces the same message as the Savior's teaching: 'acquire my peace within yourselves ... for the child of true Humanity exists with you. Follow it! Those who seek for it will find it.' ... the Gospel of Mary focuses instead on Jesus as a teacher and mediator of divine revelation. The Savior teaches that at death, the human body dissolves into the elements out of which it came; only the spiritual soul is immortal and lives forever. This knowledge leads people to discover the truth about themselves—that they are spiritual beings made in the Image of God."[230]

Professor Pagels says, "Many scholars are now convinced that the ... Gospel of John probably was written at the end of first century, emerged from an intense debate over who Jesus was or is. ... comparing Gospel of John with the Gospel of Thomas, which may have been written at about the same time ... John's gospel was written in the heat of controversy, to defend certain views of Jesus and to oppose others (or to dilute the influence by calling 'doubting Thomas'). ... Thomas's gospel encourages the bearer not so much to believe in Jesus, as John requires, as to seek to know God through one's own, divinely given capacity, since all are created in the image of God. For Christians in later generations, the

Gospel of John helped provide a foundation for a unified church, which Thomas, with its emphasis on each person's search for God, did not."[231]

By including the Gospel of John, the Council of Nicaea may have ensured a central place for the church and the priestly class. Instead of the Gospel of John, if the Council had included the Gospel of Thomas or the Gospel of Mary, Christianity and Hinduism would have looked similar.

***

Unlike Hinduism, Christianity gave the priests the power to forgive the sinners. This uniquely vested power greatly influenced the religion, as "sin" is the central theme of the religion.

Because a normal society has an inordinate share of sinners, the person who could forgive the sinners would carry great power and obviously a large following. This extraordinary power greatly influenced the history of medieval Europe.

Being jointly responsible for building a unified Christian society, the church and the king cooperated with each other. However, despite the mutual dependence, there was a level of mistrust.

To ensure the churches did not sway the people against the kings, the rulers preferred to appoint their own bishops in their country. However, the popes were not pleased with this encroachment on their God-given authority.

Even in the twenty-first century, reportedly, a similar tussle is developing between the Vatican and the Chinese government. Against the Vatican's great angst, the Chinese have appointed their own bishops in their Catholic churches. The Chinese regard the Vatican's insistence on appointing their bishops inside China as interference in China's internal affairs.[232]

In the Middle Ages, one such conflict pitted Pope Gregory VII against Holy Roman Emperor Henry IV of Germany. In 1075, the pope threatened the emperor with his and his family's destruction unless he stopped appointing the bishops and abbots. Upon being ignored by the emperor, the pope ordered Henry deposed and ordered that no one was to obey him. For the next couple of years Henry retaliated, but in the end lost out. Forgiveness for the sins was important; people listened to the pope rather than their rulers. Eventually, Henry waited in the snow outside the pope's castle in Canossa, Italy, begging for absolution.[233]

In 1095, when Pope Urban II launched a crusade to gain overall supremacy of Christendom, and, additionally, free Jerusalem from the Muslims, he told the Crusaders that if they died in the Crusades, they would go straight to heaven.[234]

In the fourteenth and fifteenth centuries, the popes even declared that, for the right donation, they could guarantee a straight path to heaven without any fear of purgatory. They started selling insurance against future sins.[235]

The God-given authority to forgive the sinners and the power to decide who could go directly to heaven made the popes sometimes more powerful than the kings and emperors in Europe.

If the Vedas had granted the Hindu priests similar God-given powers, Hinduism would have looked very different. For one thing, there would have been no Upanishads. Besides having none of the *darshanas*, very likely there would have been no Buddhism or Jainism.

***

The rise of Martin Luther's Protestant movement in the sixteenth century led to internal conflicts within the church, and many Europeans lost their lives.[236] As a result, the popes lost their absolute power; the church became fragmented. The popes headed only the Catholic Church.

Although some Catholics may disagree, I believe the fragmentation of the church greatly contributed to the spread of Christianity around the world.

The diminished control of the church led to great scientific and technological advancement in western Europe, resulting in European industrialization. When industrialized European Christian nations started to colonize countries around the world, it opened a new untapped market for the Christian missionaries to spread their message. While Europe was the old home of Christianity, today 63 percent of Christians live in Asia, Africa, or Latin America, and more people in the world identify themselves with Christianity than any other religion.[237]

***

I have found that just as in any faith, one can find what one looks for in the Bible. One can find a passage that sows hatred or a passage that uplifts the human race by its message of good will, peace, and harmony.[238]

"An eye for an eye," revenge, envy, anger, sloth, gluttony, lust, greed, and pride are basic human instincts. The great *rishis* of the Vedas and the *darshanas*, Mahavira, Buddha, Confucius, Lao-tzu, Guru Nanak, and the Son of God do not have to come to Earth to exhort us to revert to our base instincts.

Jesus Christ preached the same Golden Rule as the others before him:

- All things whatsoever ye would that men should do to you, do ye even so to them (Christianity).[239]
- Do nothing unto others, which might cause you pain if it were done to you (Hinduism).
- Do not hurt others in a way that you would find hurtful. Seek for others the happiness you desire for yourself (Buddhism).
- Never do to others what you would not like them to do to you (Confucianism).

I believe Jesus is asking us to uplift ourselves from our base instincts, free ourselves from the seven deadly sins, and develop inner purity so that we can be worthy of his grace. The Bible says, "Blessed are the pure in heart: for they shall see God."[240]

I believe the Christian "pure in heart" and Hinduism's "inner peace" are not that far apart.

Just as the Hindus speak of the soul, C. S. Lewis, a highly respected twentieth century figure in Christian circles, speaks of the presence of divinity within us. He says, "The Christian thinks any good he does comes from the Christ-life inside him. When Christians say the Christ-life is in them ... they mean that Christ is actually operating through them. ... Christians are Christ's body, the organism through which He works."[241]

Hinduism talks about the soul and the Supreme Soul. The way to the Supreme Soul is through the soul because they are the same. The core message from Jesus appears identical:

> I and my Father are one.[242]
> ...the Father is in me, and I in him.[243]
> Jesus saith unto him, I am the way, the truth, and the life:
> no man cometh unto the Father, but by me.[244]

From the psalms of Christianity, "Mark the perfect man, and behold the upright: for the end of that man is peace. ... Peace be within thee," to the wisdom of Hinduism, all stress the inner peace.[245]

The following passages from the Bible are not very different from Hinduism's *tat twam asi*:

> So God created man in his own image; in the image of
> God created He him ...[246]
> The Spirit of man is the candle of the Lord ...[247]
> The kingdom of God is within you.[248]
> ...your body is the temple of the Holy Ghost which is in
> you...[249]
> ...ye are the temple of the living God...[250]

***

Mother Teresa, the feeble-looking nun in a white *sari* and open sandals, the winner of the Nobel Peace Prize in 1979, and one of the Vatican's leading candidates for sainthood, said, "Do not look for Jesus away from yourselves. He is not out there; He is in you. Keep your lamp burning, and you will recognize Him."[251] When asked if she converted people, the devout Catholic missionary nun, who dedicated her life to Jesus, said, "Of course, I convert. I convert you to be a better Hindu or a better Muslim or a better Protestant. Once you have found God, it's up to you to decide how to worship Him."[252]

When the mind is truly enlightened, the sectarian distinctions disappear.[253] The spiritually enlightened souls see no distinctions of thine and mine in the Kingdom of Spirit.[254]

11

FUTURE

There are many faiths, but the spirit is one, in me, in you and in every man.

—Leo Tolstoy

I like the description of religion I read a long time ago. Imagine life as a beautiful novel whose first and last parts have been torn out and are missing. All the religions try to do is rewrite the novel, filling in those missing parts—why we are here and what happens when we die—with particular points to make and visions to advance.

Water droplets are pure when they start as rain, but by the time they hit the roof and reach the ground through the gutters, they can get dirty because of the medium they pass through. Similarly, religions can be defiled by the medium through which they manifest.[255]

Because of fear or ignorance, followers of one religion often regard their own beliefs, customs, and rituals as particularly holy while declaring those of others to be farcical, preposterous, and repugnant. For centuries, leaders around the world with vested interests have exploited religious differences for their political and materialistic gains, and spawned humanity's miserable history of religious warfare and persecution.

Nothing has contributed more for peace and love in the world than religion; nothing has engendered fiercer hatred than religion. Nothing has brought people closer than religion; nothing has bred more bitter enmity between people than religion. Nothing has inspired people to build more charitable institutions and hospitals than religion; nothing has deluged the world with more bloodshed than religion.[256]

The future of religions and humankind will depend on the choices we make. Only we can decide if we should use our religions to bring peace within us and in the world, or we should let our leaders exploit our religions for their vested interests and plunge all of us into an abyss.

***

I hope the increasing global interconnectedness will foster understanding and make people realize that the same spiritual thread of love, compassion, patience, tolerance, forgiveness, and inner peace permeates through all the great religions of the world.

I also hope that the Hindus around the world continue to respect all other faiths, embrace science in the pursuit of the eternal truth, be open to ideas that enrich their faith, be more spiritual in their outlook, and use their *dharma* to subdue ego, seek inner peace, and in the spirit of *ekam sat viprah bahudha vadanti* promote understanding between faiths. After all, *tat twam asi.*

> *May all be well. May there be peace for all. May all be fulfilled. May all be prosperous.*
> *May all be happy. May all be free from disease. May all realize what is good. May none be subject to misery.*
> *Om, Shanti, Shanti, Shanti.*[257]

Glossary

Abhaya mudra: hand gesture in which the palm of the deity is raised toward the devotee to inspire trust, dispel fear, and bless the devotee; gesture of fearlessness

Abhinivesa: clinging to life as if it never ends, fear of extinction

Acharya: the rules of conduct

Adharma: against *dharma*, acts that infringe on *dharma*

Aditi: boundless, Vedic goddess of unbounded space, viewed as the Great Mother of all the Vedic gods and all creation

Adityas: Aditi's sons, who include up to twelve Vedic gods such as Mitra, Varuna, Indra, and the Sun god

Advaitya (also spelled *advaita*): non-dual

Advaitya Vedanta (also spelled Advaita Vedanta): non-dual Vedanta or the Upanishad

Agamas: holy books mostly dedicated to Shiva (and his other names)

Agni: Vedic god of fire

Ahamkara: the "I-maker" or the ego

Ajna (eyebrow *chakra* or third eye, also spelled Agya): one of the Tantric *chakras*

Ambika: the mother, one of the aspects of Shakti

Amrita: no-death or eternal life; the nectar of immortality

Anahata (heart *chakra*): one of the Tantric *chakras*

Ananda: eternal bliss

Anatta: no Self

Anjali: paying homage to the god with folded hands

Ankusha: a hook; remove obstacles from the path of *dharma*; the force by which all wrongful things are repelled

Annaprasana: feeding a baby solid food, one of the rituals

Annapurna: the benevolent goddess of plenty and harvest, one of the aspects of Shakti

Antar anga: the inner limbs of Patanjali Rishi's Astanga Yoga, namely *dharana, dhyana*, and *samadhi*

Antaryamin: the internal controller

Anteshthi: the funeral rites

Apsara: seductress nymph

Aranyakas: the wilderness or the forest texts; Vedic texts associated with the *vanaprastha* phase of life

Arati: honoring the deity with light

Ardha: half

Arhat: a worthy one

Artha: wealth, material possessions, and worldly success

Arya Dharma: another name for Hinduism

Arya Samaj: another name for the Hindu society

Aryaman: Vedic god of ancestors

Asana: posture, sitting, one of Patanjali Rishi's Astanga Yoga; sitting on the fence (Artha Sastra)

Ashmita: ego

Ashrams: phases to get the faithful to shift methodically from a materialistic to a spiritual life; resting places

Astanga: eight limbs as in Patanjali Rishi's Astanga Yoga; the first five are the *Bahira Anga* or the outer limbs and the remaining three are the *Antar Anga* or the inner limbs

Astika: a believer in the Supreme

Asuras: demons

Aswa (also spelled *asva*) *medha*: horse sacrifice

Atharva Veda: one of the four Vedas

Atma (also spelled *atman*): the individual soul

Atma-aupamya: equality of others with oneself

Aum: please see *Om*

Avatar: incarnate

Avidya: ignorance of the real or the Supreme Soul

Avyaktam: without vibration, the state when the universe exists but only as potential

Bahira anga: the outer limbs of Patanjali Rishi's Astanga Yoga, namely *yama, niyama, asana, pranayama,* and *pratyahara*; also please see Astanga

Baikuntha (also spelled Vaikuntha): the abode of the gods

Bhagavad Gita: please see Gita

Bhaktas: devotees

Bhakti: devotion

Bhakti Yoga or Bhakti Marga: the devotional path, one of the paths to *moksha*

Bhava: expression

Bheda: planting dissent in the enemy's camp

Bhukti: worldly materialistic and sensual enjoyments

Bhutas: gross matter

Bodhi tree: the Tree of Wisdom

Bodhiridaya: heart of enlightenment, love, and understanding

Bodhisattva: one who has attained *nirvana* but has chosen to re-enter the cycle of *sansaar* to save other sentient beings

Brahma: the creator, aspects of Brahman, Brahma is also known as Hiranyagarbha, "the golden womb"; Prajapati, "the lord of progeny"; Pitamah, "the patriarch"; and Viswakarma, "the architect of the universe." Brahma represents universal intelligence

Brahmaloka: the world of Brahman

Brahman: the Supreme Being, and the source of everything

Brahmanas: part of the Vedas, set of prose composed to help the priests with the sacrificial rituals and the mantra recitations

Brahmins: one of four castes, focused on religious work, academia, and intellectual pursuits

Bramahcharya: the unmarried phase

Bratabandha or upanayana: a ritual to induct a young Hindu into the faith

Brihaspati: Jupiter

Bubhuksus: those who desire *bhukti*, the worldly materialistic and sensual enjoyments

Buddhi: a combination of intellect, wisdom, and discernment

Budha: Mercury

Chakra: represents multiple forms of the universe into being similar to the spin of a discus; also center of spiritual energy within a person's body as envisioned by the Tantrics

Chandra: Moon

Charvakas: materialists who believed that there was no god or afterlife, and promoted maximum materialistic and sensual pleasures in one's lifetime; Charvakas are called *bubhuksus*

Chetriyas (also spelled Kshatriyas): the group that focused on the affairs of the state, called Rajanya in the Veda; one of the castes

Chit: consciousness

Chitta-vritti-nirodha: the suppression of the fluctuations of mind as in Patanjali Rishi's Yoga

Daana: donation or charitable giving

Dalits: the oppressed; also please see Harijans

Dama: gift or bribe

Damaru: rhythm of creation and dissolution; the sound at the beginning of the Creation

Danavs: demons

Danda: punishment

Darshana: spiritual perception acquired by intuitive experience sustained by logical arguments and critical expositions

Deva: god

Devi: goddess

Dham: sacred site

Dharana: intense concentration on an object, one of Patanjali Rishi's Astanga Yoga

Dharma: a combination of moral duty, ethics, a vehicle to hold together or bind all living beings in a harmonious order, and the essence

Dhyana: meditation, one of Patanjali Rishi's Astanga Yoga

Diksha: an initiation ritual using *mantras* under the direction of a guru

Diwali (shortened version of Dipawali, also spelled Deepavali, Deepawali, and Dipavali): a major Hindu festival, also known as the Festival of Lights

Dukkha: suffering, anguish

Durga: the goddess who destroys evil, one of the aspects of Shakti

Dvaitya (also spelled *Dvaita*): dual

Dvaitya Vedanta (also spelled Dvaita Vedanta): considers *atma* as completely and eternally distinct from God

Dwesa: aversion

Dyaus: Vedic god of the sky

Ekam sat viprah bahudha vadanti: Truth is one, wise call it by various names

Gada: a force that will overwhelm

Gaja-hasta mudra: a gesture in which the left foot is raised to show that all those who approach with devotion will find *moksha*

Gaja Lakshmi: the goddess, who is seated on lotus while being showered with water from pots wielded by a pair of elephants, one of the aspects of Shakti

Ganapati: please see Ganesh

Ganesh: a god whom the Hindus worship before worshipping other gods; also known as Vinayaka, the remover of obstacles in the universe, the god who clears obstacles from the path of *dharma;* as Ganapati, he is the leader of the demigods

Ganga Maata: Mother Ganga

Gauri: the fair-complexioned goddess, one of the aspects of Shakti

Gayatri Mantra: one of the verses from the Rig Veda used in daily prayers

Ghanta: bells

Gita: the Divine Song, one of the most revered and venerated books in Hinduism

Gopinis: dairymaids

Gopura: gateways

Gopurams: please see *Gopura*

Grihasthi: the householder

Gunas: qualities; combination of three essential characteristics: *Sattwa, Rajas, Tamas*

Gurmukh: one devoted to God

Gurudwara: the door to the guru, Sikh's place of worship

Gyana: knowledge

Gyana Yoga or Gyana Marga: path of knowledge, one of the paths to *moksha;* called Sankhya Yoga in the Gita

Halahala: please see *Kaalakuta*

Harijans: the children of God; also please see *Dalits*

Havan: please see *Homa*

Hiranyagarbha: the golden womb, another name for Brahma

Homa: oblations to the sacred fire in a ceremonial fire pit

Indra: a Vedic god, thunderbolt-wielding warrior king and ruler of the heavens, god of cloud and rain

Indrajala: conjuring or trickery

Indriyas: centers of sense perception

Ista devatas: related or friendly gods

Itihasa: history

Jaati: caste

Jagad Mata: the world mother, one of the aspects of Shakti

Janeu: sacred thread

Japa: chant holy names

Jina: the victorious one

Jinja: shrine

Jivanmukta: one who attains *mukti* while still alive

Jivanmukti (turiya): *mukti* while still alive

Jivatma (also spelled *jivatman*): individual soul; please also see *Atma*

Jnana Yoga: please see Gyana Yoga

Kaal: time, death

Kaalakuta: a poison that could have killed the entire creation

Kaarana: the casual state

Kali: the goddess who destroys evil, one of the fierce aspects of Shakti

Kalpa: Brahma's day or the twelve-hour cycle, 4.32 billion Earth years

Kama: pleasures of the senses

Kameshawari: the goddess of erotic love, one of the aspects of Shakti

Karma: the consequence of every action and every thought

Karma saaya: *karmic* residues

Karma Yoga or Karma Marga: path of action, one of the paths to *moksha*

Karuna: compassion and feel others' pain

Ketu: descending node of the Moon

Khalsa: the pure

Khandas: parts

Klesas: impairments of the mind and affliction that perpetuate *karmic* bondage

Krishna: one of the *avatars* of Vishnu

Kshatriyas: please see Chetriyas

Kubera: Vedic god of wealth

Kundalini: the infinite creative energy of the Supreme Being that resides in every human (Tantric)

Lakshmi (also spelled Laksmi or Laxmi): the goddess of wealth and prosperity, Vishnu's consort, one of the aspects of Shakti

Lalitha: the smiling and auspicious goddess, one of the aspects of Shakti

Lalitha Tripurasundari: the auspicious and beautiful goddess of all worlds, one of the aspects of Shakti

Laxmi: please see Lakshmi

Langar: Sikhs' community kitchen attached to a *gurudwara* where they prepare and serve free food

Linga: male sexual organ

Maha: great, major

Maha kalpa: dissolution of the universe, 311 trillion Earth years

Maha Tripurasundari: the great beautiful goddess of all worlds, one of the aspects of Shakti

Mahadeva: the great god, another name for Shiva

Mahadevi: the great goddess, one of the aspects of Shakti

Mahakavyas: great epics

Mahalaksmi: the great Lakshmi, one of the aspects of Shakti

Maharishi: a great *rishi*

Maheswor: the great god, another name for Shiva

Maitri: friendship and loving kindness toward others

Manana: critical thinking

Manas: the mind processing the thoughts

Manava: humankind

Mandalas: circles

Mandir: a temple

Mangala: Mars

Manipura (solar plexus *chakra*): one of the Tantric *chakras*

Manmukh: one attached to the worldly life

Mantra: free oneself from the active mind, a combination of two words, *manas*, and *trai*, "to free from"; also please see *Saguna mantra* and *Nirguna mantra*

Marga: path

Maya: illusion superimposed on the spiritual reality due to one's ignorance; deceit (Artha Sastra)

Moksha or *mukti*: connection with the Supreme Soul and liberation from the cycle of rebirth

Mudita: find joy in others' happiness

Mudra: a gesture

Mukta: one who has attained *mukti* or *moksha*

Mukti: please see *Moksha*

Muladhara (base *chakra*): one of the Tantric *chakras*

Mumuksus: those who desire *moksha*

Muni: eminent sage; an alternative name for a *rishi*

Murali manohar: the handsome one with a flute

Murti: sculpture

Naag: the king of the snakes

Namakarana: naming a child, one of the rituals

Narga: hell

Nastika: a nonbeliever in the Supreme

Nataraja: an aspect of Shiva

Navagrahas: nine heavenly bodies

Neti, neti: not this, not that

Nididhyasana: meditating on the Self

Nigama: one of the *Tantras*

Nirakara: without form, gender, or other physical characteristics

Nirguna: without the *gunas*

Nirguna mantra: a *mantra* that has no reference whatsoever to a god

Nirvana: a state of utmost tranquility, total silence, absolute peace and quiet, or total serenity

Nivritti marga: path of renunciation

Niyama: self-discipline, internal control, calmness, one of Patanjali Rishi's Astanga Yoga

Nyaya: one of the six *darshanas*

Om (Aum): the first sound that occurred when the universe was created; Brahman's symbolic representation

Om tat sat: *Om* that is the truth

Paap: demerit, sin, a wicked or an evil act

Paddhatis: ancillary texts to *agamas*

Padma: lotus

Panchasila: five moral principles

Param: supreme

Paramguru: guru's guru

Paramahamsa (also spelled Paramhansa): a title bestowed on those who have attained the supreme degree of spiritual perfection

Parikrama: please see *Pradakshana*

Parinirvana: the death of the physical body of a person who has already attained *nirvana*

Parvas: occasions or events

Parvati: Shiva's consort (also called Uma), who represents the gentler aspects of femininity, beauty, fidelity, and a dutiful loving wife, one of the aspects of Shakti

Pashupati: the pre-Vedic lord of animals in the Yoga position

Patanjali Rishi's Astanga Yoga: one of the most popular Yogas

Pipal (also spelled *peepul, peepal*): a variety of tree found mostly in the Indian subcontinent

Pitamah: the patriarch, another name for Brahma

Praan (also spelled *prana*): the energy of the soul

Pradakshana: going around the deity's *murti*

Prajapati: the lord of progeny, another name for Brahma

Prakriti: the source of the primal elements and the forces, the source of the universe and everything in it

Pralaya: end of Brahma's day and dissolution of life on Earth

Pranayama: breathing techniques, one of Patanjali Rishi's Astanga Yoga

Prasad: something that is imbued with the deity's grace

Prasthana-traya: the three foundations namely the Upanishads, the Brahma Sutra, and the Gita

Pratyahara: control the senses, to shut out the outside world, one of Patanjali Rishi's Astanga Yoga

Pravritti marga: path of worldly life

Prithvi: Vedic goddess of Earth

Pryaschittas: reparations for infringements of *dharma*

Puja: worship

Purans (also spelled Puranas): old or ancient traditions

Punya: meritorious deed, virtuous act

Purna: full

Purusarthas: the goals of life, namely *dharma, artha, kama,* and *moksha*

Purusha: the soul (Sankhya/Upanishad); God who is the source of everything animate and inanimate (Vedic)

Purva Mimamsa: one of the six *darshanas*

Raahu: the ascending node of the Moon

Raga: attachments

Rajanya: please see Chetriyas (also spelled Kshatriyas)

Rajarajeswari: the queen of the kings, one of the aspects of Shakti

Rajas: one of the *gunas*; the repulsive force, excitable energy, always active, restlessness

Rakhi: sacred thread

Rakhsasas: demons known for their extreme cruelty and for terrorizing humans

Rama: one of the *avatars* of Vishnu

Rama naam satya hai: Rama's name is the truth; the chant is a reminder that Rama is the manifestation of Brahman, who is the *sat*, the ultimate truth

Rasa: melody

Richas: Vedic passages

Rig Veda: the most prominent of the four Vedas

Rishis: eminent sages

Rudra: Vedic god of storms; one of the names of Shiva

Rudraksha: rosaries of berries from a shrub of the same name

Sachkand: a blissful state beyond the continuous cycles of rebirth

Sadhana: spiritual practice

Sadhus or *sanyasis*: ascetics

Saguna: with *gunas*

Saguna mantra: a *mantra* that refers to a god

Sahasrara (crown *chakra*): one of the Tantric *chakras*

Sakara: one with the form, gender, and physical characteristics of a human

Saligram: a smooth rounded stone containing fossilized ammonite

Sama: appeasement

Sama Veda: one of the four Vedas

Samadhi: final realization and attainment of *moksha*, one of Patanjali Rishi's Astanga Yoga

Samhitas: the hymns, the original core of the Vedas; Vaishnavism holy books

Samkhya: please see Sankhya

Samsara: please see *Sansaar*

Samskara: an impression on the mind

Samundra mathan: mythical churning of the ocean

Sanatana Dharma: eternal *dharma*; another name for Hinduism

Sani: Saturn

Sankha: conch shell; sound associated with the Creation of the universe similar to *Om*; symbol of victory over disorder

Sankhya: one of the six *darshanas*

Sankhya Yoga: please see Gyana Yoga

Sansaar: the world of a continuous cycle of life followed by death

Sanskara: tradition

Sanyas: a life of deep spiritual contemplation with total renunciation of materialistic attachments

Sanyasis: please see *Sadhus*

Saraswati: Brahma's consort; the goddess who is the epitome of universal intelligence, wisdom, creativity, learning, literature, arts, and music; one of the aspects of Shakti

Sari: dress worn by women mostly in the Indian subcontinent

Sastras: authoritative treatises on specialized topics

Sat: the ultimate truth

Sati: wife immolating herself voluntarily or under duress on the funeral pyre of her dead husband

Satsanga: keeping company of the wise

Sattwa (also spelled *sattva*): one of the three *gunas*; state of equilibrium, in balance, free, calm, serene

Satya Loka: the world of Truth

Shakti: the energy aspect of Brahman; the feminine aspect of the Supreme that sustains the universe

Shanti: peace, tranquility of mind

Shantosha: contentment

Shava: corpse

Shiva: destroyer aspects of Brahman

Shraddha: anniversary death rites

Shravana: hearing

Shruti: heard

Shunyata: a state of utmost tranquility, total silence, absolute peace and quiet, or total serenity; also please see *Nirvana*

Sloka (also spelled *shloka*): hymn that rhymes

Smriti: remembered

Sridevi: the auspicious goddess, one of the aspects of Shakti

Srishti: the beginning of Brahma's day when the living beings on Earth are created

S*thiti*: Brahma's day when the living beings on Earth exist; 4.32 billion Earth years

Sthula sharira: physical body

Stotra (also spelled *stotram*): prayer or a devotional literature related to a deity

Stridhana: a woman's personal property

Sudras: one of the castes

Sukra: Venus

Sukshma sharira: subtle or finer body

Surya: Vedic Sun god; Sun

Sutras: concise statements of principles or truths

Swadhisthana (sacral *chakra*): one of the Tantric *chakras*

Swami: master or lord; an honorific title bestowed on a guru of great wisdom

Swarga: heaven

Swastika: a symbol normally associated with the goddess of wealth and prosperity

Taal: rhythm

Tamas: one of the *gunas*; inertia, force of contraction, resistance, dense, dissolute

Tandava: dance of Shiva as Nataraja

Tanha: craving, desire

Tanmatras: the fine particles

Tantras: Tantrics' holy books

Tapa: intense form of ascetic practice and meditation

Tat twam asi: you are That

Tejas: the fiery energy that will incinerate the universe in an instant

Tika: an auspicious colorful mark on the forehead

Tilak: please see *Tika*

Tirtha: a ford or a crossing; the crossing to the heavens from a connecting point on Earth

Tirthankaras: the pathfinders

Tirthayatra: pilgrimage to a sacred place that connects to the heavens

Tribeni sangam: confluence of the three rivers

Trimurti: the triad of creator, preserver, and destroyer

Tripundra: three ash (*bivuti*) lines on people's forehead as a reminder of the transient nature of life

Trisul: trident; represents the three aspects of Brahman

Turiya: please see *Jivanmukti*

Tyaga: renounce, including property

Uma: please see Shakti

Upa: minor

Upagamas: ancillary texts to *agamas*

Upanayana: please see *Bratabandha*

Upanishad: one of the six *darshanas*

Upayas: methods

Upeksha (also spelled *upeksa, upekka*): ability to remain peaceful and calm in any crisis; remaining calm, taking no notice, ignoring (Artha Sastra)

Ushas: Vedic goddess of dawn

Uttara Mimamsa: latter critical inquiry; one of the six *darshanas*

Vaikuntha: please see Baikuntha

Vaishesika: one of the six *darshanas*

Vaishyas: one of the castes

Vanaprastha: going to the forest

Varadan mudra: a gesture in which the palm of the hand is turned toward the viewer and the fingers point down to show that the deity can grant the devotee's wishes; also please see *Mudra*

Varna: skin color; caste

Varuna: Vedic god of the skies, the custodian and enforcer of the universal law and order

Vasana: fragrance

Vayu: Vedic god of wind

Vedanta: the end of the Vedas; the Upanishads

Vedas: books of higher knowledge; foundations of Hinduism

Vedic Dharma: another name for Hinduism

Veena: an Indian stringed instrument

Vichara: rational investigation of the truth

Vidya arambha: beginning of learning, one of the rituals

Vinayaka: please see Ganesh

Vishishta Advaitya: qualified non-dual

Vishnu: preserver aspect of Brahman; one of the *trimurti*; originally a Vedic solar god closely allied with Indra

Vishuddha (throat *chakra*): one of the Tantric *chakras*

Viswakarma: the architect of the universe, one of the names for Brahma

Vivah: marriage rituals

Vyavahar: the civil and criminal law to administer justice

Yagya (also spelled as *yajna*): an elaborate form of *homa*

Yajur Veda: one of the four Vedas

Yama: Vedic god of death

Yama: inner restraint, not to hurt living beings, one of Patanjali Rishi's Astanga Yoga

Yantra: a symbol or an instrument to invoke astrological, spiritual, or magical powers

Yoni: female sexual organ

Yugas: the ages

Acknowledgement

It all started on a cold and foggy morning in the fall of 1968 in front of Big Ben and the Houses of Parliament. I was a young eighteen-year-old excited to be in London after having won a four-year full scholarship from the British government to study aeronautical engineering in England.

After giving me and other foreign students a tour of the great British institution, a guide arranged by the government had just stopped in front of Parliament, near Big Ben, when half a dozen or so families who were waiting to take us to their homes for lunch greeted us warmly. It appeared as if it were a coordinated event, as there was one family for each student. The other students from different parts of the world were also in England to study, courtesy of the British government.

My host family was a young couple, possibly in their early thirties, with two kids probably around five or six. I was impressed that they were waiting in the bitter cold to welcome a foreign student to their home. We packed into their family car; with the heater in full blast, we headed to their home on the outskirts of London.

After having a delicious home-cooked meal for lunch, we moved to the living room. They told me about British life in general, and how they got involved in hosting foreign students for lunch through their church. The couple also told me about their work and the importance of family and faith in their lives, and wanted to know about my upbringing, my faith, and my understanding of Christianity.

While growing up in Nepal, I just followed the rituals without thinking much about the religion. Not only did I not know much about Christianity, but I also did not know much about my own ancestral faith.

As I could not carry on an intelligent conversation about my faith, all I could do was ramble incoherently.

The London experience and my incoherent rambling had left an indelible impression on my mind. I promised myself to learn more about my own faith, and to also explore Christianity.

Because Hinduism is not a proselytizing religion, it has no need to hone the message or create easy-to-follow steps to attract new converts to the faith. Moreover, the flexibility within Hinduism can sometimes be overwhelming; its philosophical reasoning can be excessively subtle and often intellectually profound. Although it is my ancestral faith and I was raised into it, I found getting to the crux of Hinduism more challenging than I anticipated.

I am greatly indebted to the authors and writers, family and friends, and colleagues, who have enriched my knowledge of Hinduism and Christianity.

This book is my humble effort to capture the essence of Hinduism. I have tried to simplify the faith without compromising the core concepts. I have also tried to explore the common thread that connects Hinduism with Buddhism and Christianity. I hope this book will foster understanding between faiths.

Mohan R. Pandey
www.aPathToInnerPeace.com
aPathToInnerPeace@gmail.com

Notes

[1] Although Hinduism's holy books refer to the Supreme as Brahman, Hindus in their daily lives normally address the Supreme by different names such as Brahmatma, Paramatma, Parameshwara, Paramshiva, Parabrahma, Purusottama, Rama, Krishna, Shiva, Shakti or just *Om tat sat.* To make it easy for the readers, wherever appropriate, I address the Supreme as the Supreme Soul.

[2] Brahman is the Supreme. Not to be confused with the god Brahma (one of the aspects of Brahman), or Brahmin—the class of people that, for centuries, focused on religious work, academia, and intellectual pursuits.

[3] City of Harappa was located on the banks of the Ravi River, and Mohenjodaro by the Indus River.

[4] Amartya Sen, *The Argumentative Indian* (New York: Farrar, Straus and Giroux, 2005) p. 310.

[5] Title: Astadhyai, "Eight Chapters."

[6] Jawaharlal Nehru, *The Discovery of India* (New Delhi: Oxford University Press, 2003) p. 115.

[7] Swami Vivekananda, *The Science & Philosophy of Religion* (Kolkata: Advaitya Ashrama, 2002) p. 41; based on Swami Vivekananda's class talk "A study of the Sankhya Philosophy" in New York, on January 8, 1896.

[8] Wendy Doniger, *The Hindus: An Alternative History* (New York: The Penguin Press, 2009) p. 306.

[9] Ibid., p. 340.

[10] S. Radhakrishnan, *Indian Religions* (New Delhi: Orient Paperbacks, 1983) p. 100.

[11] S. Radhakrishnan, *Indian Philosophy, Volume* 1 (New Delhi: Oxford University Press, 2004) p. 67.

[12] Rig Veda 10.64.15, translated by Ralph T. H. Griffith (1896).

[13] Manusmriti 5.39.

[14] Ralph T.H. Griffith, translation, *Sacred Writings Hinduism: The Rig Veda* (New York: Quality Paperback Book Club, 1992) p. ix.

[15] Heinrich Zimmer, edited by Joseph Campbell, *Philosophies of India* (New York: Pantheon, 1953) p. 9.

[16] *Rita* appears synonymous with the "Grand Unified Field Theory and Theory of Everything" where Quantum Mechanics and Theory of Relativity merge. So far, the Grand Unified Field Theory and Theory of Everything is only a concept in modern science.

[17] Rig Veda includes other deities such as Aditi—the mother, Dyaus—god of the sky, Prithvi—goddess of Earth, Surya—Sun god, Ushas—goddess of dawn, Kubera—god of wealth, Yama—god of death, Vayu—god of wind, and Aryaman—god of ancestors. Aditi, which means "boundless," is the Vedic goddess of unbounded space, and viewed as the Great Mother of all the gods and all creation. Adityas are her sons, who include up to twelve gods such as Mitra, Varuna, Indra, and the Sun god.

[18] The essence of Rig Veda 3.62.10, part of Gayatri Mantra in Sanskrit: "*tat savitur varenyam bhargo devasya dhimahi dhiyo yo nah prachodayat.*" Savitur is synonymous with the Sun and respresents the Sun's divine vivifying power—the energy aspect that enlivens, stimulates, animates, and illuminates.

[19] Ralph T.H. Griffith, translation, *Sacred Writings Hinduism: The Rig Veda* (New York: Quality Paperback Book Club, 1992) p. ix.

[20] *Ashram* also means a resting place.

[21] S. Radhakrishnan, *Indian Philosophy, Volume 1* (New Delhi: Oxford University Press, 2004) pp. 43-44.

[22] In Sanskrit: *nam kritwa ghrtam pibet, yavaj jivet sukham jivet; bhsami bhutesya dehesya kutah punar agamano bhavet.*

[23] Some scholars speculate that the real name of the founder of Vaishesika *darshana* was Kasyapa Rishi. Kanada, which also means "atom-eater," was a descriptive name given to the nature of the Vaishesika *darshana*.

[24] S. Radhakrishnan, *Indian Philosophy, Volume 2* (New Delhi: Oxford University Press, 2004) p. 177.

[25] Rig Veda 10.90, translated by Ralph T. H. Griffith (1896).

[26] Rig Veda 10.129, translated by Ralph T. H. Griffith (1896).

[27] S. Radhakrishnan, *Indian Philosophy, Volume 1* (New Delhi: Oxford University Press, 2004) p. 141.

[28] All quotations attributed to the Gita in this book are based on the Gita's original passages in Sanskrit, their various translations in English such as *The Bhagavadgita or The Song Divine* (Gorakhpur: Gita Press, 2001); S. Radhakrishnan, *The Bhagavadgita* (New Delhi: Blackie & Son (India), 1977); W. J. Johnson, *The Bhagavad Gita* (Oxford: Oxford University Press, 1994); Jack Hawley, *the Bhagavad Gita* (California:

New World Library, 2001); A. C. Bhaktivedanta Swami Prabhupada, *Bhagavad-Gita, As It Is* (Los Angeles: The Bhaktivedanta Book Trust, 1989); Stephen Mitchell, *Bhagavad Gita* (New York: Three Rivers Press, 2000); Juan Mascaro, *The Bhagavad Gita* (Middlesex: Penguin Books, 1971); P. Lal, *the Bhagavadgita* (New Delhi: Orient Paperbacks, 1983).

[29] Wendy Doniger, *The Hindus: An Alternative History* (New York: The Penguin Press, 2009) p. 104; A.L.Basham (Kenneth G. Zysk, ed.,), *The Origins and Development of Classical Hinduism* (New York: Oxford university Press, 1989) p.20.

[30] Rig Veda 1.164.46.

[31] S. Radhakrishnan, *The Bhagavadgita* (New Delhi: Blackie & Son (India), 1977) p. 293; A dilemma faced by Dattatreya nearly three thousand years ago in his Avadhutgita, a collection in praise of Brahman. Dattatreya was the son of a great *rishi* Atri, hence "atreya." Dattatreya was a great spiritual teacher, whom some Hindus worship as the incarnation of Brahman.

[32] Dialogs and debates between learned King Janaka and his famous teacher, the legendary *rishi*, Yagnavalkya (also spelled Yajnavalkya). A king of proverbial wisdom and righteousness Janaka, who was Sita's father, ruled the ancient Kingdom of Videha from Mithila, now known as Janakpur, which is in Nepal. The Brihadaranyaka Upanishad mentions women who participated in the discussions such as Gargi Vachaknavi as mentioned in Brihadaranyaka Upanishad 3.6 and 3.8, and Maitreyi, wife of the legendary *rishi*, Yagnavalkya, as mentioned in Brihadaranyaka Upanishad 2.4 and 4.5.

[33] Brihadaranyaka Upanishad 1.3.28; in Sanskrit: *Asato ma sat gamaya, tamaso maa jyotir gamaya, mrityor maa amritam gamaya.*

[34] Many Upanishads include both verse and prose.

[35] Isa Upanishad 8, 4, and 5.

[36] Chandogya Upanishad 6.8.7.

[37] Brihadaranyaka Upanishad 2.5.19.

[38] Mundaka Upanishad 2.2.5: Swami Paramananda, *Four Upanishads* (Chennai: Sri Ramakrishna Math, 2006) p.134.

[39] Katha Upanishad 2:18: Swami Paramananda, *Four Upanishads* (Chennai: Sri Ramakrishna Math, 2006) p. 53.

[40] Brihadaranyaka Upanishad 4.4.5–7, dialog between the legendary *rishi*, Yagnavalkya, and King Janaka.

[41] Katha Upanishad 3.3–4.

[42] Katha Upanishad 4.1.

[43] Svetasvatara Upanishad 6.1–12.

[44] Brihadaranyaka Upanishad 3.7.2, 3.7.16, and 3.7.20.

[45] Swami Paramananda, *Four Upanishads* (Chennai: Sri Ramakrishna Math, 2006) p. 33.

[46] Ibid., p. 19.

[47] Based on: Swami Nirvedananada, *Hinduism at a Glance* (Calcutta: Ramakrishna Mission, 2002) p. 243.

[48] S. Radhakrishnan, *Indian Philosophy, Volume 1* (New Delhi: Oxford University Press, 2004) p. 49.

[49] Bhagavad Gita is also called *Bhagavad-gitopanishad*, "Upanishad Sung by the Lord."

[50] S. Radhakrishnan, *Indian Philosophy, Volume 1* (New Delhi: Oxford University Press, 2004) p. 524.

[51] Gita 6.32.

[52] Maitrayani Upanishad 4.5 assimilates Brahma, Vishnu, and Rudra into Brahman.

[53] It has its origins in Rig Veda 10.125 verse 8, which identifies Shakti as the energy aspect of the Supreme. The verse says, "I breathe a strong breath like the wind and tempest, the while I hold together all existence." (Translated by Ralph T. H. Griffith (1896)). Alternative translation: "I wander like the wind bringing forth all things." (S. Radhakrishnan, *Indian Philosophy, Volume 1* (New Delhi: Oxford University Press, 2004) p. 487).

[54] D. S. Sarma, *Hinduism Through the Ages* (Bombay: Bharatiya Vidya Bhavan, 1989) p. 20.

[55] Ibid., p. 25.

[56] Ibid., pp. 36–37.

[57] Ibid., p. 42.

[58] Commonly known in the West as ISKCON.

[59] D. S. Sarma, *Hinduism Through the Ages* (Bombay: Bharatiya Vidya Bhavan, 1989) p. 44.

[60] A.L. Basham, *The Wonder that was India* (New York: Grove Press, 1959) p. 333.

[61] Stephen Cross, *The Elements of Hinduism* (Dorset: Element Books, 1996) p. 87.

[62] Catholics in India believe that the St. Thomas Mount in Chennai, India contains the remains of the apostle.

[63] William Manchester, *A World Lit Only By Fire* (Boston: Little, Brown, 1993) pp. 7–8.

[64] http://en.wikipedia.org/wiki/parsi, October 12, 2012.

[65] Swami Venkatesananda, *Vasistha's Yoga* (New York: State University of New York Press, 1993) pp. 175–6, Passage 4.36.

[66] Ibid., p. 176, Passage 4.37.

[67] Ibid., p. 180, Passage 4.40.

[68] Muslim population (approx.) as a percentage of total population (approx.): 13.4% of India's 1.21 billion, 89.7% of Bangladesh's 148 million, 1% of Bhutan's 743,000, 4% of Nepal's 27 million, 97% of Pakistan's 177 million, and 8% of Sri Lanka's 21 million.

[69] D. S. Sarma, *Hinduism Through the Ages* (Bombay: Bharatiya Vidya Bhavan, 1989) p. 61.

[70] Hindu literatures speak of *stridhana*, "woman's personal property," which included mostly jewelery, clothing, and money. Although it could be used by the husband in case of dire emergency, for all practical purposes *stridhana* was her own, and when she died it normally passed on to her daughters.

[71] Rig Veda 10.90, translated by Ralph T. H. Griffith (1896).

[72] Mahabharata: Vanaparva verse 311. In response to a question from Yaksha, Yudhishthira says that, without doubt, it is not birth, not study, not learning, only the conduct that makes one a Brahmin.

[73] Jawaharlal Nehru, *The Discovery of India* (New Delhi: Oxford University Press, 2003) p.120.

[74] Stephen Cross, *The Elements of Hinduism* (Dorset: Element Books, 1996) p. 15.

[75] People in Bali, who have been practicing Hinduism for nearly two-thousand years, do not have the concept of untouchable caste.

[76] R. J. Unstead, *A History of the World* (London: Book Club Associates, A&C Black, 1984) p. 155.

[77] Wendy Doniger, *The Hindus: An Alternative History* (New York: The Penguin Press, 2009) pp. 577–578; similar conclusion: A.L. Basham, *The Wonder that was India* (New York: Grove Press, 1959) p. 481.

[78] Prince William of the United Kingdom married a "commoner," Catherine Middleton, on April 29, 2011. A future king marrying a commoner was considered a break with tradition and made major headlines. Miss Middleton did not come from a royal or an aristocratic background.

[79] Bubonic plague in the fourteenth century killed nearly one-third to one-half of the population of Europe.

[80] Mahatma Gandhi, *The Spirit of Hinduism* (New Delhi: Pankaj Publications, 1980) p. 71; Stephen Cross, *The Elements of Hinduism* (Dorset: Element Books, 1996) p. 16.

[81] As mentioned earlier, the essence of Rig Veda 3.62.10, part of Gayatri Mantra in Sanskrit: "*tat savitur varenyam bhargo devasya dhimahi dhiyo yo nah prachodayat.*" Savitur is synonymous with the Sun, respresents the Sun's divine vivifying power—the energy aspect that enlivens, animates, and illuminates.

[82] *The American Heritage Dictionary of the English Language, 3rd edition* (New York: Houghton Mifflin Company, 1992).

[83] http://en.wikipedia.org/wiki/File:Three_Handed_Virgin_of_Troyan_Monastery.JPG, October 14, 2012.

[84] Discussed in Chapter "Elements," under "Holy Books," "Purans."

[85] Ibid.

[86] Kaustubha is a divine jewel. According to Hindu legends this was the fourth of fourteen rare gems recovered during the mythical churning of the ocean (*samundra mathan*) at the beginning of time while searching for the nectar of immortality, *amrita*.

[87] Hindus often quote the following Sanskrit passages from Gita 4.7 and 4.8: *Yada yada hi dharmasya glaanir bhavati Bharata, abhyu thanam dharmasya tadatmanam srija myaham, pari tranaya sadhunam binasaya cha duskritam, dharma samsthapanarthaya sambhabaami yuge yuge.*

[88] *Sayings of Sri Ramakrishna: An Exhaustive Collection* (Madras: Sri Ramakrishna Math, 2006) p. 32.

[89] The holiest Hindu temples dedicated to Vishnu or one of his other forms/ *avatars* as shown inside the parentheses are in Badrinath in the state of Uttarakhand, Puri (Jagannath) in the state of Orissa, Tirupati (Venkatesa/Balaji) in the state of Andhra Pradesh, Trivandrum (Padmanabh) in the state of Kerala, and Dwarika (Krishna) in the state of Gujarat. All these states are in India.

[90] Apasmara Purusha is the demon, who represents the demon of ignorance. *Bhaktas* who created the Nataraja sculptor show Apasmara Purusha as a dwarf.

[91] Hindus worship Shivalinga as Shiva (or one of his 108 other names) and Parvati in many temples such as the ones at Amarnath, Kedarnath, Rameshwaram (worshipped as Ramanathaswamy), Varanasi (worshipped as Vishwanath), near Veravali in Gujarat (worshipped as Somanath), near Nasik (worshipped as Trimbakeshwar), and Kathmandu (worshipped as Pashupatinath). In Chidambaram, they worship Shiva as Nataraja. Except for the temple of Pashupatinath in Kathmandu, Nepal, these temples are located in India in the states shown in parentheses: Amarnath (Jammu and Kashmir), Kedarnath (Uttarakhand), Rameshwaram (Tamil Nadu), Varanasi (Uttar Pradesh), Veravali (Gujarat), Nasik (Maharastra), and Chidambaram (Tamil Nadu).

[92] Using the Biblical passages (such as Revelation 20:10), a sermon of eternal damnation for those who do not repent and follow Christ. It uses the vivid imagery of burning in hell for eternity.

[93] Rig Veda identifies her as Vak, "speech personified," later associated with Saraswati

[94] Book review by Sam Miller, "Stranglers of the Night," *India Today International,* June 6, 2005; book by Mike Dash, *Thug: The True Story of India's Murderous Cult* (London: Granta Books, 2005).

[95] Vishnu Puran, Book 2, Chapter 6.

[96] Brihadaranyaka Upanishad 4.4.6.

[97] Heavens above Bhurloka, "earth," in ascending order of bliss: Bhuwarloka, Swarloka, Janaloka, Maharloka, Tapaloka and Satyaloka. Hells below Bhurloka, "earth,"

in increasing order of suffering: Atalaloka, Vitalaloka, Sutalaloka, Rasatalaloka, Talatalaloka, Mahatalaloka and Patalaloka.

[98] Scholars list 92 such books on Shaivism (normally called *agamas*) dedicated to Shiva and his other names: 10 Shiva, 18 Rudra, and 64 Bhairava; 77 on Shaktism (normally called Tantras); and 108 on Vaishnavism (normally called Samhitas such as Vaishnava Pancharatra Samhitas). Some of the holy books have other ancillary texts. For example, *agamas* have ancillary texts called *upagamas* and *paddhatis*, which further elaborate the *agamas*.

[99] According to the Puran, the Satya Yuga lasts for 4,800 years of demigods, the Treta Yuga for 3,600 years of demigods, the Dwapara Yuga for 2,400 years of demigods, and the Kali Yuga for only 1,200 years of demigods. Hence, one cycle of the four Yugas is 12,000 years of demigods. Because the demigods live on a different plane, a year of the demigod is 360 Earth years. Hence, one cycle of the four Yugas, or one *Maha Yuga* is 4.32 million Earth years. One thousand cycles of the *Maha Yugas*, which is 4.32 billion Earth years, equals Brahma's twelve hours. The living beings on Earth are created (*srishti*) at the beginning of Brahma's day, exist (*sthiti*) for 4.32 billion Earth years, and dissolve at the end of Brahma's day (*pralaya*). The living beings disappear during Brahma's twelve-hour night or 4.32 billion Earth years before the Brahma's *kalpa* or the *srishti-sthiti-pralaya* starts all over again.

[100] Hindu literature speaks of *maha kalpa* or the dissolution of the universe when Brahma gets to a hundred years of age, which translates into 311 trillion Earth years. Brahma has thirty 24-hour days in a month and twelve months in a year. Brahma's 24-hour day is 8.64 billion Earth years.

[101] Among the eighteen Maha Purans, Brahma, Brahmanda, Brahma-Vairava, Markandeya, Bhavisya, and Vamana are associated with Brahma. Vishnu, Bhagavata, Narada, Garuda, Padma, and Varaha are associated with Vishnu. Vayu or Shiva, lnga, Matsya, Kurma, Skanda, and Agni or Agneya are associated with Shiva.

[102] The story of Manu is similar to the story of Noah from the Book of Genesis from the Bible and the story of the flood from the Sumerian epic of Gilgamesh. Very likely, it is a description of the same flood, whose devastation must have had a great impact on the surrounding civilizations.

[103] Baudhayana statements 1.45–1.48 in the Sulba Sutra.

[104] Stephen Hawking and Leonard Mlodinow, *The Grand Design* (New York: Bantam Books, 2010) p. 19.

[105] S.Radhakrishnan, *Our Heritage* (New Delhi: Orient Paperbacks, 1984) p. 15. In Sanskrit: *na jatu kamah kamanam upabhogena samyati havisa krsnavartmeva bhuya evabhivardhate.*

[106] A.L. Basham, *The Wonder that was India* (New York: Grove Press, 1959) p. 50.

[107] Pandavas were the five sons of King Pandu: Yudhisthira, Bhima, Arjuna, Nakul, and Sahadeva. Kauravas, which means "the descendants of Kuru," were the one hundred sons of King Dhritarastra. Kurus were the royal ancestors of Pandavas and Kauravas. Duryodhana was the eldest of the Kauravas.

[108] Sir Monier Monier-Williams, *Brahmanism and Hinduism or Religious Thoughts and Life in India as based on the Veda and other Sacred books of Hinduism* (New York: Macmillan and Co., 1891) p. 389; A translation with nearly similar sentiments appears in A.L. Basham, *The Wonder that was India* (New York: Grove Press, 1959) pp. 181-182.

[109] Literal translation of *itihasa*: "thus (*iti*) indeed (*ha*) it was (*asa*)."

[110] Mahatma Gandhi, *The Spirit of Hinduism* (New Delhi: Pankaj Publications, 1980) p. 49-51.

[111] Ibid.

[112] Emperor Ashoka's sense of revulsion after the battle for the Kingdom of Kalinga discussed later in this book, in Chapter, "Hinduism and other Faiths," under "Buddhism."

[113] Ibid.

[114] Some of the festivals (including some, which are the same festivals but called by different names by the different communities): Basanta Panchami, Saraswati Puja, Makar Sakranti, Pongol, Maha Shiva Ratri, Holi, Ram Navami, Hanuman Jayanti, Rath Yatra, Teej, Rishi Panchami, Guru Purnima, Naag Panchami, Raksha Bandan, Indra Jatra, Gai Jatra, Krishna Janmastami, Ganesh Chaturthi, Navaratri, Durga Puja, Bijaya Dashami, Diwali, Bhai Tika, Vivah Panchami.

[115] Not to be confused with "*samskara*," the impression on the mind from *karma*.

[116] All major religious traditions have rites-of-passage rituals similar to *upanayana* or *bratabandha*; for example, the Christians have baptism and the Jews have Bar Mitzvah.

[117] Although Hindu holy books speak of learned women, they did not leave their homes to study at the guru's house. It appears that groups whose primary function was to take care of others were exempt from the rituals of *upanayana*, and hence the requirements of the *bramahcharya phase*. It included Sudras whose natural duties according to Gita 18.44 were the services of others, and women who were expected to take care of their husbands and children. It appears that for women and Sudras, marriage was the ritual that inducted them formally into the faith.

[118] Hindu *navagrahas* include: *surya* (Sun), *chandra* (Moon), *mangala* (Mars), *budha* (Mercury), *brihaspati* (Jupiter), *sukra* (Venus), *sani* (Saturn), *raahu*, and *ketu*–the ascending and descending nodes of the Moon.

[119] Many Hindus prepare an astrological chart for their newborn. Based on the time of birth, priests calculate the positions of the *navagrahas* and compile an astrological

chart for the newborn. Some Hindus believe that the position of the *navagrahas* can affect one's fortunes and health, and consult with the priest to review the astrological chart before embarking on major initiatives.

[120] S. Radhakrishnan, *Indian Religions* (New Delhi: Orient Paperbacks, 1983) p. 58.

[121] *Pipal*, botanical name: *ficus religiosa*; even Gita 15.1–3 refer to the *pipal* tree (asvattham); Buddha attained *nirvana* after meditating for forty-nine days under the *pipal* tree, later called the *bodhi* tree or the Tree of Wisdom. Archaeologists believe that the spear-shaped leaves seen in the seals found in Mohenjodaro were leaves from the *pipal* tree.

[122] The duration of the Kumbha Mela fluctuates (as it is based on the lunar calendar). Some in the media appear to use Maha interchangeably with Purna. Some even contend that the 2001 Kumbha Mela was a Purna Kumbha Mela and the 2013 Kumbha Mela was the Maha Kumbha Mela. Regardless, Hindus consider all Kumbha Melas holy.

[123] Badrinath (Uttarakhand) in the north, Rameshwaram (Tamil Nadu) in the south, Jagannath Puri (Orissa) in the east, and Dwarika (Gujarat) in the west. These are the four holy places established by Adi Shankaracharya in the eighth century A.D.

[124] Regional groups of holy places such as the Char Dham in the Himalayan group, called Chota (smaller) Char Dham: Badrinath, Kedarnath, Gangotri, and Yamunotri. All four are in the state of Uttarakhand in India. The Mahabharata mentions seven *dhams*: Varanasi, Mathura, Ujjain, Hardwar, Prayag, Ayodhya, and Gaya. Hindus also consider Ayodhya, Dwarika, Hardwar, Kanchipuram, Mathura, Ujjain, and Varanasi as the seven holy cities. Based on the Puranic myths, there are anywhere from four to 108 sacred locations for Shakti that *bhaktas* call Shakti Pithas. These are mostly located in Nepal and the northern regions of India such as Bengal and Rajasthan. In addition, there are many other holy places. These include the network of twelve Shiva temples with Shivalingas known as the Shaiva Jyotirlinga networks, Vaishnava sites associated with Rama and Krishna, and the regional networks such as the Murukan-Palani associated with six temple pilgrimage centers in Tamil Nadu.

[125] In Sanskrit: *yatha ichhasi tatha kuru*.

[126] S. Radhakrishnan, *Indian Religions* (New Delhi: Orient Paperbacks, 1983) p. 136.

[127] The Bible, Galatians 6:7.

[128] S. Radhakrishnan, *Recovery of Faith* (New Delhi: Orient Paperbacks, 1984) p. 96.

[129] Some also refer to *sukshma sharira* as *ativahika sharira*.

[130] Not to be confused with "*sanskaras*," "traditions," as in Hindu *sanskaras*.

[131] Swami Venkatesanada, *Vasistha's Yoga* (New York: State University of New York Press, 1993) p. 28, Passage 2.9.

[132] Ibid., pp. 26 and 28; passages 2.5, 2.8, and 2.9.

[133] In Sanskrit: *Ya drishi bhaawana yashya siddhir bhawati ta drishi.*

[134] Khaptad Swami, Bichar Bigyan (Kathmandu: His Majesty's Government of Nepal, 1977) p. 93.

[135] *Jivanmukta* is one who has attained *jivanmukti*, "*mukti* while still alive." Some refer to *jivanmukti* as *turiya.*

[136] In Sanskrit: *Chhadasya kadasya chaiva bidyamartha cha saadhayet, chhada tyage kuto bidya kada tyage kuto dhanam.*

[137] Swami Adiswarananda, *The Four Yogas* (Vermont: Skylight Paths Publishing, 2006) pp. 46 and 51.

[138] Alice Calaprice, ed, *The Expanded Quotable Einstein* (New Jersey: Princeton University Press, 2000) p. 149.

[139] In Sanskrit: *Griheeta iba keshesu mreetyuna dharma macharet.* Mahatma Gandhi's saying "Live as if you were to die tomorrow, learn as if you were to live forever" was probably based on this old Hindu saying.

[140] *Tantras* include details of Tantric ritualistic worship, and address Shakti in her many forms. *Tantras* are usually in the form of dialogues between Shiva and Parvati. *Agamas* and *Nigamas* are two types of *Tantras*. It is called *agama* when Shiva is answering Parvati's questions and *nigama* when Parvati is answering Shiva's questions.

[141] Swami Vidyatamananda, ed., *What Religion Is in the Words of Swami Vivekananda* (New Delhi: Advaita Ashrama, 2004) p.1.

[142] Gita 17.24–25. Hinduism also speaks of *tyaga,* "renounce, including property."

[143] Accepted by the Hindus for centuries, now also a legal definition of Hinduism established by the Supreme Court of India in 1966.

[144] In Sanskrit: *na paape prati paapah syaat.*

[145] Fareed Zakaria, *The Post-American World, Release 2.0* (New York: W. W. Norton & Co., 2011) p. 172.

[146] Jim Remsen, "Religion Didn't Keep Hindus from Loving Her," *The Seattle Times,* September 14, 1997, p. A1.

[147] Stephen Knapp, *The Secret Teachings of the Vedas. The Eastern Answers to the Mysteries of Life, Volume one* (Michigan: The World Relief Network, 1993) p. 22.

[148] *Ashrams* in this context means "resting places," another definition of *ashrams* was "phases."

[149] Philip Goldberg, *American Veda: From Emerson and the Beatles to Yoga and Meditation—How Indian Spirituality Changed the West* (New York: Harmony Books, 2010) pp. 210–211, "Freedom lovers in guru-centered movements willingly gave up freedoms they would have scratched and clawed to protect in the outside world. ... Many grew

cynical and resentful when they discovered chicanery or incompetence on the part
of spiritual leaders whom they'd placed on the highest of pedestals. And some were
deeply wounded by a guru's betrayal of his own moral standards."

[150] Stephen Cross, *The Elements of Hinduism* (Dorset: Element Books, 1996) p. 105.

[151] Paramhansa Yogananda, *Autobiography of a Yogi* (New York: The Philosophical Library, 1946).

[152] http://www.yogananda-srf.org/Aims_and_Ideals.aspx#.UNVG6Gfcg-0, December 20, 2012.

[153] Julia Boorstin, "Is Yoga the Key to a Killer Golf Swing," *Fortune*, October 31, 2005, p. 198, reported on the creative use of Yoga to attract new business: "The luxury resort and spa ... will launch a $5,000 four-night program called Mindful Golf, which will teach golfers to concentrate and minimize stress through Yoga meditation."

[154] Yoga has come a long way since the 1989 Vatican document signed by Cardinal Ratzinger, who became His Holiness Pope Benedict XVI. In December 1989, the Vatican issued a document saying the practice of Eastern traditions like Yoga "can degenerate into a cult of the body," warning Catholics against mistaking Yoga's "pleasing sensations" for "spiritual well-being." The Vatican's position on Yoga and Zen meditation was published in *The Congregation for the Doctrine of the Faith*, December 1989, signed by Cardinal Ratzinger and approved by Pope John Paul II. The Vatican sees the declaration as an attempt to elaborate on guidelines for proper Christian prayers rather than a condemnation of the Eastern meditation practices such as Yoga and Zen. Lisa Cullen, "Stretching for Jesus," *Time*, September 5, 2005, wrote, "Christian Yoga is gaining a devout following ... called Yogadevotion ... is part of a fast growing movement that seeks to retool the 5000 year old practice of Yoga to fit Christ's teachings. ... It draws potential converts through the church's doors; about a quarter of Yogadevotion students are not churchgoers."

[155] Aum Shinrikyo, which means "Supreme Truth," was a Japanese group founded by Shoko Asahara in 1984. "[It] is a syncretic belief system that incorporates Asahara's idiosyncratic interpretations of Yoga with facets of Buddhism, Hinduism, Christianity, and the writings of Nostradamus." [http://en.wikipedia.org/wiki/Aum_Shinrikyo, February 1, 2012.]

Aum is an alternative spelling for the Hindu *Om*; Shinrikyo roughly means "religion of Truth." "In 1984, Asahara returned from a visit to India and told his disciples that he had attained Boddhi (enlightenment). His closest disciples offered him money, which he could now accept, and Asahara used this money to organize an intensive Yoga seminar that lasted several days and attracted many people." [http://en.wikipedia.org/wiki/Shoko_Asahara, February 1, 2012.]

"It attracted such a considerable number of young graduates from Japan's elite universities that it was dubbed a 'religion for the elite.'" Asahara outlined a doomsday prophecy; humanity would end, except for the elite few who joined Aum Shinrikyo. He claimed that he would take away their sins and bad *karma*. In 1995, reportedly, the group claimed they had more than nine thousand members in Japan and as many as forty thousand worldwide. Some believe that such groups normally attract people who are looking for something different and, once caught up in the group dynamics, find it difficult to challenge the beliefs for fear of social reprisal from their fellow group members. The group gained international notoriety when it carried out a coordinated Sarin gas attack on five trains in the Tokyo subway on the morning of March 20, 1995, killing thirteen commuters, seriously injuring fifty-four, and affecting possibly as many as five thousand people. [http://en.wikipedia.org/wiki/Aum_Shinrikyo, February 1, 2012.]

[156] For example, the modern scientific findings do not appear to support the timing and sequence of the Creation in Genesis (Chapter 1).

[157] Examples of passages from the Bible implying the Earth is flat and the center of the universe: "Earth cannot be moved" (Psalm 93.1), "four corners of Earth" (Isaiah 11:12 and Revelation 7:1), "... the Earth abideth forever. The Sun also ariseth, and he Sun goeth down, and hasteth to his place where he arose." (Ecclesiastes 1:4-5).

[158] Stephen Hawking and Leonard Mlodinow, *The Grand Design* (New York: Bantam Books, 2010) p. 22.

[159] Ibid., p. 41.

[160] Ibid., p. 124.

[161] The Bible, Genesis 1.

[162] Based on new data, some scientists suggest that the universe is 13.8 billion years old.

[163] Allen Boyce Eddington, ed., *Essential Einstein* (California: Pomegranate Art Books, 1995) p. (v).

[164] Shri Ram Verma, *Vedas: the Source of Ultimate Science* (Delhi: Nag Publishers, 2005) p. 164; Rig Veda 10.5.6.

[165] Ibid., p.162; Rig Veda 10.149.1.

[166] Ibid., p. 164; Rig Veda 1.84.15.

[167] Wendy Doniger, *The Hindus: An Alternative History* (New York: The Penguin Press, 2009) p. 372.

[168] Amartya Sen, *The Argumentative Indian* (New York: Farrar, Straus and Giroux, 2005) pp. 28–29.

[169] A.L. Basham, *The Wonder that was India* (New York: Grove Press, 1959) p. vi;

On pp.495-496, A.L. Basham writes, "Through the necessity of accurately laying out the open-air site for a sacrifice Indians [the word Indians can be interchanged with the word Hindus] very early evolved a simple system of geometry, but in the sphere of practical knowledge the world owes most to India in the realm of mathematics ... The success of Indian mathematics was mainly due to the fact that the Indians had a clear conception of abstract number ... with the aid of a simple numeral notation, devised a rudimentary algebra, which allowed [Indians] more complicated calculations than were possible to the Greeks ... the earliest inscription recording the date by a system of nine digits and a zero, with place notation for the tens and hundreds ...The name of the mathematician who devised the simplified system of writing numerals is unknown, but [it was before] the 4th century A.D. ... For long, it was thought that the decimal system of numerals was invented by the Arabs, but this is certainly not the case. The Arabs themselves called mathematics 'Indian (art)' (*hindsat*)..." A.L. Basham adds, "Medieval Indian mathematicians ... made several discoveries which in Europe were not known until the Renaissance or later. They understood the import of positive and negative quantities, evolved sound systems of extracting square and cube roots, and could solve quadratic and certain types of indeterminate equations. For ϖ [pi] Aryabhata gave the usual modern approximate value of 3.1416 [later expanded to nine decimal places] ... The mathematical implications of zero (*shunya*) and infinity, never more than vaguely realized by classical authorities [in Europe], were fully understood in medieval India." Indians had proved that a number divided by zero was infinity. A.L. Basham says, "[It] had been recognized in Indian theology at least a millennium earlier, that infinity, however divided, remains infinite ..."

Jawaharlal Nehru, *The Discovery of India*, (Oxford University Press: New Delhi, 1985) p. 116-117: "In mathematics the ancient Indians made some epoch-making discoveries, notably that of the zero sign, of the decimal place-value system, of the use of the minus sign, and the use in algebra of letters of the alphabet to denote unknown quantities. ... Ten formed the basis of enumeration in India even at the time of the Rig Veda. The time and number sense of the ancient Indians was extraordinary. They had a long series of number names for very high numerals. The Greeks, Romans, Persians, and the Arabs had apparently no terminology for denominations above the thousand or at most the myriad ($10^4=10,000$). In India there were eighteen specific denominations, and there are even longer lists. In the story of Buddha's early education, he is reported to have named denominations up to 10^{50}. At the other end of the scale, there was a minute division of time of which the smallest unit was approximately one-seventeenth of a second, and the smallest lineal measure is given as something, which approximates to 1.37x7⁻¹⁰. All these big and small figures were no doubt entirely theoretical and used for philosophical purposes. … Even their mythology deals with ages of hundreds of millions of years…. The popular mind in Europe was used to a time scale which did not go beyond a few thousand years."

170 S. Radhakrishnan, *The Present Crisis of Faith* (New Delhi: Orient Paperbacks, 1983) p. 17.

171 Jawaharlal Nehru, *The Discovery of India* (New Delhi: Oxford University Press, 2003) p. 558.

172 Allen Boyce Eddington, ed., *Essential Einstein* (California: Pomegranate Art Books, 1995) p. 20.

173 Jawaharlal Nehru, *The Discovery of India* (New Delhi: Oxford University Press, 2003) p. 188, quoting Swami Vivekananda.

174 S. Radhakrishnan, *Indian Religions* (New Delhi: Orient Paperbacks, 1983) p. 11.

175 Jawaharlal Nehru, *The Discovery of India* (New Delhi: Oxford University Press, 2003) pp. 187–188, quoting Swami Vivekananda.

176 Chandogya Upanishad, 3.19.1 to 4.

177 http://en.wikipedia.org/wiki/Georges_Lema%C3%AEtre, January 7, 2012.

178 A.L.Basham (Kenneth G. Zysk, ed.,), *The Origins and Development of Classical Hinduism* (New York: Oxford university Press, 1989) p.128.

179 Some cosmologists believe that stretching of the universe was actually decelerating until about 4.5 billion years ago.

180 "Double Dark" theory suggests that stretching of the universe accelerated when the dark energy surpassed the gravitational attraction of the dark matter. The theory suggests that dark energy's repulsive force increases with the increasing stretching of the space, and hence the acceleration.

181 Brian Greene, "The Mystery of the Multiverse," *Newsweek*, May 28, 2012, pp. 23–24.

182 Michael Shermer, *The Believing Brain* (New York: Times Books, 2011) p. 5.

183 Joel R. Primack and Nancy Ellen Abrams, *The View from the Center of the Universe: Discovering our extraordinary place in the cosmos* (New York: Riverhead Books, 2006) p. 208.

184 Ibid., p. 186, quoting Erwin Schrodinger from his book: *What is Life?* (1958; repr. Cambridge University Press, 1967).

185 Discussed in Chapter "Elements," under "Holy Books," "Purans" of this book.

186 Jill Bolte Taylor, *My Stroke of Insight* (New York: Viking, 2006) p. 18.

187 Some publications list humans and chimpanzees share 98.4 percent of DNA.

188 Jill Bolte Taylor, *My Stroke of Insight* (New York: Viking, 2006) p. 133.

[189] Sharon Begley, "How Thinking Can Change the Brain," *The Wall Street Journal*, January 19, 2007, p. B1; the article quoted Professor Richard Davidson, University of Wisconsin–Madison.

[190] Michio Kaku, *Physics of the Future* (New York: Doubleday, 2011) p. 202.

[191] A.L. Basham, *The Wonder that was India* (New York: Grove Press, 1959) p. 257.

[192] Queen Maya is also known as Queen Maha Maya, Queen Maya Devi; Prajapati also known as Maha Prajapati. Prajapati is a Sanskrit spelling, in Pali they drop the 'r,' and call her Pajapati.

[193] There are many versions of what the astrologers said. However, they can be summarized to two: Siddhartha would conquer the world and be a Universal Emperor or he would become an enlightened sage who would devote his life to helping others overcome their suffering and be a Universal Teacher.

[194] Amartya Sen, *The Argumentative Indian* (New York: Farrar, Straus and Giroux, 2005) p. 321; Gregorian year 2000 equals 6001 in the Kaliyuga calendar, 2544 in Buddha Nirvana, 2057 in Vikram Sambat, 1922 in Saka, 1921 Vedanga Jyotisha, 1407 in Bengali San, and 1176 in the Kollam calendar.

[195] It is very likely that the Buddha Nirvana Calendar is based on Buddha's *nirvana* instead of his *parinirvana*. If it were based on his *parinirvana*, that would put Buddha's birth at 624 B.C. This would make Buddha older than Jain's Mahavira, who was born in 599 B.C. All available literatures speak of Mahavira being an elder contemporary of Buddha.

[196] Dharmapada 1.

[197] Dharmapada 100.

[198] Dharmapada 5.

[199] Dharmapada 223.

[200] Dharmapada 104.

[201] S. Radhakrishnan, *Indian Religions* (New Delhi: Orient Paperbacks, 1983) p. 170, quoting Buddhacarita, XI, 64.

[202] Jawaharlal Nehru, *The Discovery of India* (New Delhi: Oxford University Press, 2003) p. 128.

[203] S. Radhakrishnan, *Recovery of Faith* (New Delhi: Orient Paperbacks, 1984) p. 174.

[204] Jawaharlal Nehru, *The Discovery of India* (New Delhi: Oxford University Press, 2003) p. 120.

[205] S. Radhakrishnan, *The Spirit of Religion* (New Delhi: Hind Pocket Books, 2000) p. 57.

[206] S. Radhakrishnan, *Our Heritage* (New Delhi: Orient Paperbacks, 1984) p. 10.

[207] Jawaharlal Nehru, *The Discovery of India* (New Delhi: Oxford University Press, 2003) p. 172.

[208] Mahayana started in northwest India at the time of Kanishka, who was an Indian emperor around the second century A.D. whose empire extended all the way to the current northwest regions of Pakistan and parts of Afghanistan. Many Buddhists see Kanishka as a great patron of the faith.

[209] Gita 2.72.

[210] Dharmapada 5.

[211] Patanjali Rishi's Yoga Sutra 1.33: Edwin F. Bryant, *The Yoga Sutras of Patanjali* (New York: North Point Press, 2009) p. 481

[212] Mandukya Upanishad 3:1.1–5, 7.

[213] Monastic centers, "maths" (states in parentheses): Sringeri (Karnataka), Puri (Orissa), Dwarika (Gujarat), and Jyotirmath near Badrinath (Uttarkhand) started by Adi Shankaracharya in the eighth century A.D.

[214] S. Radhakrishnan, *Indian Religions* (New Delhi: Orient Paperbacks, 1983) p. 173.

[215] It appears that this receptiveness was not confined only to the faiths that sprouted in the East. The Italian explorer Marco Polo's writings suggest that this openness extended to faiths from the West such as Christianity. Marco Polo wrote that the Great Kublai Khan, in the thirteenth century A.D., sent a letter to Pope Clement IV asking him to send a hundred "learned men" to teach his people in China about Christianity. Even the ferocious Genghis Khan, who probably practiced some form of Tantric Buddhism, allowed freedom of religion in the lands he conquered.

However, the receptiveness had its limits. When Catholic missionaries started making inroads in Japan and, rather than enriching the ancestral faith of Japan, they preached replacing the ancestral belief system with Christianity, the Japanese reacted in a different manner. According to Monica Duffy Toft, Daniel Philpott, Timothy Samuel Shah (*God's Century: Resurgent Religion and Global Politics*, New York: W. W. Norton & Company, 2011, p. 63), "The Tokugawa or Edo period (1603–1868) saw the Japanese regime prohibit Catholicism and marshal Buddhism as an instrument of state power."

[216] Although there were occasional conflicts, periods when a ruler gave preference for one faith over the other, for most of the last two millennia these faiths appear to have coexisted peacefully.

[217] Ibid., p. 31; quoting J. Estlin Carpenter: *The Place of Christianity in the Religions of the World*, p. 60.

[218] C. Scott Littleton, general editor, *Sacred East* (California: Duncan Baird Publishers Ltd., 1996) p. 160.

[219] Ibid.

[220] V. S. Ramachandran, *The Tell-Tale Brain: A neuroscientist's quest for what makes us human* (New York: W.W. Norton & Company, 2011) p. 124.

[221] Jalal-ud-din Muhammad Rumi, *Masnavi III*, p. 12.

[222] Verses recited by Mahatma Gandhi: *Ishwara allah tera naam, mandir masjid tere dham, sabako sanmati de bhagawaan.*

[223] Jon Meacham, "The Birth of Jesus," *Newsweek*, December 13, 2004, p. 58.

[224] David Van Biema, "Lost Gospels," *Time*, December 22, 2003, pp. 55–61.

[225] Jay Tolson and Linda Kulman, "The Real Jesus," *U.S. News & World Report*, March 8, 2004, p. 43.

[226] Thomas Cahill, *Pope John XXIII* (New York: Viking, 2002) p. 7.

[227] The Bible, Romans 6:23.

[228] Elaine Pagels, *The Gnostic Gospels* (New York: Vintage Books, 1989) p. 120: "In 367, Athanasius, the powerful Archbishop of Alexandria, sent an order to purge all 'apocryphal books' with 'heretical tendencies.'"

[229] Elaine Pagels, *Beyond Belief: The Secret Gospel of Thomas* (New York: Random House, 2003) p. 177; Pagels speculates that monks near the town of Nag Hamadi who heard of the order removed more than 50 books from the monastery library, hid them in a jar to preserve them, and buried them near the cliffs where they were found after centuries.

[230] Karen L. King, *The Gospel of Mary of Magdala* (California: Polebridge Press, 2003) pp. 31, 37.

[231] Elaine Pagels, *Beyond Belief: The Secret Gospel of Thomas* (New York: Random House, 2003) p. 34.

[232] Editorial, *South China Morning Post*, Jan. 22, 2007.

[233] Terry Jones and Alan Eraira, *Crusades* (London: Penguin Books, 1996) pp. 6–7.

[234] Jay Tolson and Linda Kulman, "The Real Jesus," *U.S. News & World Report*, March 8, 2004, p. 45.

[235] William Manchester, *A World Lit Only By Fire* (Massachusetts: Little, Brown, 1993) p. 40.

[236] Karen Armstrong, *The Battle for God* (New York: Alfred A. Knopf, 2000) p. 75.

[237] Joane O'Brien, Martin Palmer, *The Atlas of Religion* (California: University of California Press, 2007).

[238] For example, even the Bible has passages of hatred such as: Joel 3:10, "Beat your plowshares into swords, and your pruninghooks into spears"; Joshua 6:21, "And they utterly destroyed all that was in the city, both man and woman, young and old, and ox, and sheep, and ass, with the edge of the sword"; Matthew 10:34, "Think not that I

[Jesus] am come to send peace on earth: I came not to send peace, but a sword." The Bible also has passages that uplift the masses and spread the message of peace such as Matthew 5–7, "The Sermon on the Mount."

239 The Bible, Matthew 7:12.

240 The Bible, Matthew 5:8.

241 C. S. Lewis, *The Case for Christianity* (New York: Touchstone, 1966) pp. 54–55.

242 The Bible, John 10:30.

243 The Bible, John 10:38.

244 The Bible, John 14:6.

245 The Bible, Psalms 37:37 and 122:8.

246 The Bible, Genesis 1:27.

247 The Bible, Proverbs 20:27.

248 The Bible, Luke 17:21, Acts 17:27, Matthew 5:8.

249 The Bible, I Corinthians 6:19.

250 The Bible, II Corinthians 6:16.

251 Becky Benenate and Joseph Durepos, eds., *No Greater Love–Mother Teresa* (California: New World Library, 1997) p. 21.

252 Ibid., p. 22; Same quotes also appear in: Jim Remsen, "Religion Didn't Keep Hindus from Loving Her," *The Seattle Times*, September 14, 1997, p. A20.

253 Ramakrishna Paramhansa, a saint, perceived by some as the God incarnate.

254 S. Radhakrishnan, *Indian Religions* (New Delhi: Orient Paperbacks, 1983) p. 71.

255 *Sayings of Sri Ramakrishna: An Exhaustive Collection* (Madras: Sri Ramakrishna Math, 2006) p. 288.

256 Swami Vivekananda, *A Study of Religion* (Kolkata: Advaita Ashrama, 2004) p. 88 (based on Swami Vivekananda's presentation in the Universalist Church, Pasadena, California, January 28, 1900).

257 In Sanskrit:

Sarvesham swastir bhavatu.
Sarvesham shantir bhavatu.
Sarvesham purnam bhavatu.
Sarvesham mangalam bhavatu.
Sarve bhavantu shukhina.
Sarve shantu niramaya.
Sarve bhadrani pashyantu.
Ma kashchid dukkha bhaga bhavet.
Om, Shanti, Shanti, Shanti.

Index